The
Invisible Fist

The
Invisible Fist
Secret Ninja Methods of Vanishing Without a Trace

ASHIDA KIM

A Citadel Press Book
Published by Carol Publishing Group

A Citadel Press Book
Published by Carol Publishing Group
Citadel Press is a registered trademark of Carol Communications, Inc.

Editorial, sales and distribution, rights and permissions inquiries should be addressed to
Carol Publishing Group, 120 Enterprise Avenue, Secaucus, N.J. 07094.

In Canada: Canadian Manda Group, One Atlantic Avenue, Suite 105, Toronto, Ontario
M6K 3E7

Carol Publishing Group books may be purchased in bulk at special discounts for sales
promotion, fund-raising, or educational purposes. Special editions can be created to
specifications. For details, contact Special Sales Department, Carol Publishing Group,
120 Enterprise Avenue, Secaucus, N.J. 07094.

Manufactured in the United States of America

10 9 8 7 6 5 4 3 2 1

Library of Congress Cataloging-in-Publication Data

Kim, Ashida.
    The invisible fist : secret Ninja methods of vanishing without a
trace / Ashida Kim.
        p. cm.
    "A Citadel Press book."
    ISBN 0-8065-2018-3
    1. Ninjutsu. I. Title.
UB271.J3K5597   1998
355.5'48—dc21   98–23400
                                                        CIP

"I cannot describe to you the indescribable, but I can teach you several by no means inconsiderable arts—invisibility, flying without wings, invulnerability to sword or serpent's fang—you know the kind of thing. Here, then, is your syllabus of study. Seeking the mysterious portal, you must first provide yourself with the wherewithal to bribe the guards and render yourself invisible that you may slip through unnoticed. That sort of thing is not mastered in a day. Next, you will have to learn to fly henceforth to the courts of heaven, make your way to the central chamber, surprise Lord Lao at breakfast, snatch up his flask of golden elixir, slay those who will come running to rescue it, break down the walls of the sky-castle and return to earth an immortal! A man of your determination has but to follow my course of instruction to be certain of success."

—from the Nei Pien of Ko Hung, an ancient treatise on alchemy, medicine, and religion, 320 A.D.

Contents

Preface

The Invisible Fist cannot be seen. It gives no warning, nor can it be stopped. You cannot hide from it, nor can you escape it. Why is this so?

Some martial arts teach that a punch must be so swift and return so quickly that it is faster than the human eye can follow. Any decent self-defense class can teach one to draw up his courage in the face of danger, the better to execute one all-out, totally committed, do-or-die technique.

If the body can move faster than the eye, however, it can also react faster. The old magician's claim that "the hand is quicker than the eye" applies equally to defender and attacker. So, no matter how fast you are, no matter how many hours or years you may have spent training yourself to react to an attack with an appropriate block, you still cannot hit or block what you cannot see. Thus, the true Invisible Fist would be one that cannot be seen. It gives no warning and cannot be deflected. One cannot hide from it because those who have the secret do not go around showing it off. If it is encountered, it is due to one's own bad karma in looking for a fight with a master.

Nor can one escape the wrath of the Invisible Fist, since it is brought upon oneself by bad conduct. In this way, those who would commit evil attract the very forces that will mete out appropriate justice to them.

That is why, at certain periods in history, those who practiced this art were known as the Black Dragon Tong of Retribution, not because they went around like Robin Hood, "righting wrongs and punishing evil doers," but because they were simple, humble people who were often mistaken for victims. If they could not escape, they were, and are today, quite capable of destroying an attacker in order to survive. Also, being humble, knowing that the taking of a life does no one honor, they would take no credit for such acts, though they obeyed the ancient samurai injunction to have the power to "kill and walk away." That is because the followers of this system are so inoffensive that at one time the founders thought themselves in such harmony with nature that they would limit the number of footsteps they made each day so as not to disturb the earth with their presence. The rule is: first, do no harm; second, never make a challenge; third, never turn down a challenge.

Bullies, muggers, rapists, and the like often have a long history of crimes, violent or otherwise. So when a criminal's body is found, it is frequently taken for granted that an old enemy must have caught up with him and extracted some measure of revenge, for surely, only one as brutal, ruthless, and deadly as the villain himself could have overcome him.

This is not always so. What of the kind? The weak? The aged? Are they to have no defense except force, which they are often ill-inclined or unable to employ with enough skill to be effective? Should they be armed, even with nonviolent types of weaponry, which can be taken away from them and used by an attacker, making a weapon as dangerous for the user as for the victim? Or, should they simply resign themselves to being sheep, preyed upon by the more aggressive and assertive wolves, fleeced and butchered at the whim of those less worthy, who contribute nothing to the welfare of the tribe and, in fact, greatly contribute to its downfall by their inappropriate behavior? No, they need not.

When martial arts such as Karate, Kung Fu, and so on were first introduced to America, two claims were made about them:

that *anyone* could overcome any attacker, and could do so *without physical contact.*

Regardless of size, age, or infirmity, one need never again fear assault, because these systems made it possible to control a fight long before it began, and, if the initiative was lost due to a surprise attack, take it back from even a ferocious and aggressive enemy—but all required that the user stand and fight.

Ninjitsu, the Invisible Fist, is the only martial art that is not about fighting; it is about running away and hiding. It is about good health and longevity. It is about patience, because all true masters know that living well is the best revenge. Thus, it is by explaining the method whereby the promises made by those who would commercialize it are fulfilled.

All martial arts and their philosophies agree that the greatest warrior is the one who wins without fighting. In the classic martial arts film *Enter the Dragon,* the late Bruce Lee illustrated this principle when he confronted a brutish bully's challenge. He told this lout that his own style was the "art of fighting without fighting," but that he would need more room than the small ship they were on to demonstrate it properly. He thus enticed the bully to board a small boat so they could go to a nearby island. Once the bully was in the lifeboat, Lee simply slipped the mooring line free and held him at his mercy by threatening to set him adrift in the turbulent seas. He had won without throwing a single punch: He had outwitted his opponent.

In the television series *Hanto Yo,* about the American Indians, the mystic-warrior, the only one who dared ride a white horse into battle, the "shirt-man" and hero of the tribe, was the most adept at leading the enemy forces deep into the forest and away from his fleeing people. He single-handedly defeated the enemy by letting them wear themselves out chasing him. Once when he fought on the plains, an eclipse took place while he was charging alone toward an attacking tribe—an example of synchronicity, harmony with the Universe, just as playing hide-and-seek in the forest is an example of invisibility. This "mystic" occurence so upset and terrified the opposing tribe that the battle was never fought and the war was called off. Yet, to be such a fearsome warrior, Hanto Yo spoke always of peace and harmony among the "human beings" as the Cheyenne tribe was known to call itself.

The Shaolin monks of ancient China were also known for their serenity and love of peace, even though they were trained to "fight like ten tigers." They saw it as their duty to defend China from foreign invaders. To that end, they launched the Boxer Rebellion in 1900. The members of secret societies, such as the White Lotus sect, practiced ritualistic magic as a part of their traditional boxing art, and placed such faith in their use of Iron Body Kung Fu that many believed themselves to be impervious even to bullets. They have always been recognized as masters of the martial arts, and at the core of their study is breath control, nonviolence, and self-knowledge. In fact, part of their credo reads as follows: "When faced with imminent peril of life and limb, make no show of force. Rather, one should run away than fight."

Only when flight is no longer possible may one use force to establish, maintain, or restore order. Even then, it is taught to "avoid rather than check, check rather than block, block rather than strike, strike rather than hurt, hurt rather than maim, maim rather than kill, kill rather than be killed. For all life is precious, nor can any be replaced."

The monks were each trained in a particular animal system of fighting, depending on their body type and disposition, but all were taught meditation and the art of acting invisibly. These are the source of their great internal strength and the basis of their amazing powers. Through a series of tests and trials, which were ritualized into a rite of passage into manhood, they became mystic-warriors who could fight or disappear. The technique, however, was ancient even before they incorporated it into their system.

One of the earliest known tribes in ancient China was called the Jain. They were the greatest hunters and warriors of their era, and are even spoken of highly by the famous anthropologist Joseph Campbell in his works on older religions. They were possessed of one great secret: they knew enough to build a fire and walk through the smoke to remove the scent of man from themselves before venturing into the woods on a hunt, and upon this they based an entire philosophy of invisibility. They were the Brothers of the Smoke and, like many later arts, ritualized the secrets of their clan into ceremony. This included walking on hot coals, fire eating, smoking the pipe, and so on, and such philosophical concepts as being so in harmony with Nature that no force of man could harm them. They may yet exist. As the Invisible People, who can say from whence they came or if they have ever left or even if they are still among us.

The
Invisible Fist

INTRODUCTION:
INVISIBILTY AS AN ART

Ninjitsu, contrary to popular belief, is not a system of unarmed combat or weapons mastery. It is not about fighting at all. It is about Invisibility.

When *Book of the Ninja* was published in 1980, it stated, "there is no magical technique to render oneself unseeable to the human eye."

Such techniques, however, do exist, and they can be learned through a series of specific exercises and tests devised by the venerable masters of the Pole Star School, circa 6000 B.C., recognized in China as the most ancient school of martial arts known to man. Furthermore, these methods are reserved only for those beyond the initiate or adept level of training.

The nature of those who teach the Secret Doctrine is to deny that it exists until all other methods have been studied, exhausted, and found lacking. Only then, when the student persists in his belief that there is more to magic than simple tricks and mumbo jumbo, only when he is ready to believe, only when he wonders what it all means instead of how it is done, then is the secret revealed.

These techniques are the basis for the Japanese Art of Invisibility known as Ninjitsu, the Silent Way. In them you will find many bits and pieces of other styles and systems. As there are only so many kicks, punches, throws, takedowns, and so on, what differentiates one style from another is little more than a matter of hard or soft presentation and a focus on a particular sort of technique, a variety of combinations, poetic or military nomenclature, and strategy. All teach essentially the same lessons, and all are part of the warrior quest. All possess some part of the Great Secret of Warriorship, because there are only five elements in combat, and the same principles apply to the art of vanishing, only the intent is different.

This set of techniques is but one of many. There is nothing new in magic, only new presentations of the same basic physical and chemical properties that have amused, entertained, and amazed man for centuries.

There are nine methods of the Black Dragon School given here, derived from the Eight Mystic Trigrams, which form the basis for the *I Ching*, the Chinese *Book of Changes*. These are divided into the Five Elements, which is the foundation of Chinese medicine from antiquity to the present. The dragon represents mystical power. The adjective *black* indicates that it is a hidden or concealed system.

There are others who have pursued and employed the techniques of invisibility—the Rosicrucians, the followers of Gnosticism, the Kahuna, wizards, witches, and shamans throughout the ages. Some vanish by rearranging the physical structure of their corporeal being so that light may pass unhindered through them. Thus they become invisible. Some disassemble themselves in an instant and reform elsewhere, safely out of harm's way. Then there are those who bend the very rays of light itself around themselves to form a shimmering cloud of obscurity that hides them from view. Finally, there are those with the power to place the idea of invisibility into the mind of the observer so that he refuses to see that which is clearly before his eyes. This is the Dragon Method of "clouding men's minds," and one means by which practical invisibility may be achieved.

To that end, here are assembled the various techniques used by the Black Dragon Ninja for making an attacker blink, hesitate, flinch, turn away, or otherwise distract him from he who wishes to be invisible, including methods which temporarily or permanently blind an opponent. Absent are the various tricks of remaining invisible, like hiding, and the methods of striking from ambush, which is a way of winning any conflict in a single devastating blow. These are considerations to be taken into account once invisibility has been accomplished.

The concern of this text is the ability to disappear. The Art of Invisibility is divided into five elements: camouflage, concealment, cover, appearing, and vanishing. These equate quite nicely with the traditional Five Elements of Chinese medicine and philosophy, on which many martial arts are also based. It is a simple and effective method of categorizing a variety of techniques into easily defined groups so they can be remembered, which also allows for the inclusion of new techniques as they are developed or discovered. Thus, the system remains consistent, yet dynamic.

This method also makes it possible to compare systems which may, at first, seem widely disparate.

The Five Elements may be mnemonically recalled at any time by using the fingers:

Earth is the little or pinky finger.
Water is the ring or third finger.
Fire is the middle finger.
Air is the index finger.
Wood is represented by the thumb.

Each represents a state of matter—solid, gas, or liquid; and a type of energy—linear, circular, or spiral. Thus, even though such primitive systems are usually discredited by modern scientists as being merely examples of allegorical reasoning, such classification, to illustrate the interaction of physical and chemical properties, altogether avoids the issue of whether matter and energy are two dissimilar states of being or are interchangable, a question which has plagued scientific minds for decades.

To the ancients, such a question was meaningless. It is not important whether matter can be created or energy destroyed. What is important is how things interact. Nor were the ancients prone, as is so often the case in recorded history, to try to discover how things worked by dissecting them. They merely observed and noted cause and effect, and developed what today are called hypothetical constructs that could be tested and validated like modern laboratory experiments. The old ones called these "patterns," and had no need for vast, complicated texts to explain them. They had only a few simple "laws," which covered them all.

In keeping with Five Element symbolism, this text is divided into five sections. This is the traditional way of presenting such material, on a scroll or scrolls, sometimes known as *tora-maki,* meaning "sacred writings." In the Hai Lung Ryu (Black Dragon School) there are many such arcane manuscripts, usually categorized by the element they are said to represent. Each of the Five Elements interacts with the others, just as their symbolic names imply, and so represents the endless cycle of growth, change, and rebirth. Each also represents what modern scientists would call one of the states of matter.

For ages it was believed that matter existed in one of three states, and that matter and energy could not be created or destroyed. This may well be true, but what does it tell us about how these states interact? The old Ninja Five Element formula explains it all, and includes even more than had been previously "discovered," such as the plasma energy level.

Earth is the most solid form of matter. It has weight and occupies space. Water is the liquid state of matter. The particles are not so tightly packed nor bound together in a shape. Air is the next, most gaseous, type of matter, in which the particles are even more widely dispersed. Fire represents the plasma state of matter, a level of transition between what are called matter and energy only recently discovered by atomic science. Wood describes the three types of motion (linear, circular, and spiral) in which these particles and their manifestations may engage: electromagnetic vibratory force acting in a circular motion about a linear axis. This is the Force.

So everything is covered, from matter to nonmatter and all degrees of vibratory existence and excitement in between, which determine the level of perception upon which they exist.

We who have studied and practice these arts have no fear that they will be learned by anyone with criminal intent or deviant moral fiber. Such persons do not have the patience to advance slowly, step by step, through the long process of study, and may even attempt advanced techniques without proper preparation or precaution, leading only to their demise. One cannot learn to be a "fire-breathing dragon" without first learning how to breathe air properly, and all war, indeed all life, is a matter of breath control.

This course of study is arranged in logical order for self-instruction. Each lesson is a building block for the next. We have found that when one studies in this manner, one advances at his own rate and level of interest, and must actively participate in the course. When one undertakes such an inner journey, one often returns "changed"—not in the sense that he is possessed of some new magical power, rather, his level of spirituality has been raised and he has been granted an appreciation of life, and others will perceive this.

Invisibility is a power man has strived for throughout the ages. Like flying, levitation, precognition, telepathy, healing, and speaking with those who have passed on, it has fascinated and intrigued the great minds of sages, alchemists, and yogis as an expression of the ability to defend oneself through nonviolence. After all, it takes two to make a fight. If only one is present, then he must eventually see that all anger is directed at the self alone, by the self alone. Frustration at the acts of others is a manifestation of ego, a projecting of one's own faults onto others. Likewise, all wounds are ultimately self-inflicted.

No one can see the future accurately. Only general trends, reflected by the heavens or the seasons, give any real semblance of precognition. So to anticipate the outcome of any future event is necessarily to build up an expectation that is unattainable. Regardless of whether we expect doom and gloom or roses and rainbows, the actual outcome of any event is never exactly as we hoped or feared. Thus, humankind has for eons set itself up for endless disappointment and frustration.

Expect nothing! Judge nothing! Each morning, like a scholar at his first class, prepare a blank mind upon which the day may write. With this single act, you can change the world.

Most psychologists would agree that the perception of reality, either as a glorious world full of hope and opportunity or a dark and sinister place where virtue is often crushed by greed, is largely a matter of perspective, and have devised some clever tests to illustrate to their patients the fallacy of their thinking, one example being "is the glass of water half full or half empty?" The pessimist sees the glass half empty, perceiving only what has been lost or consumed. The optimist sees it as half full, observing what remains.

The correct answer for a sage, or a Ninja, would be that the glass is too big for the amount of water which it is intended to contain, not a smart-aleck answer at all, although it might be seen as such by a researcher "expecting" one of the two answers he provided. Instead, what it illustrates is that the patient is capable of thinking, of reasoning, of seeing more than just two outcomes. Such is the purpose of the Buddhist koans—to make the student think! So modern psychiatry has not invented anything new with this "test," and, in fact, as given in the above example, is not even aware of how to use the technique properly.

How much easier must it be then, for a martial art to lose

sight of its past, its objectives, even its principles? Ninjitsu is translated from the Japanese to mean "the Silent Way." That is because those who practice it do not go about bragging of it to others, or even trying to share it with them, until such time as they themselves ask. The Invisible Fist is not a "secret society," it is a society with secrets.

Keep that thought before you as you study these techniques, many of which are revealed here for the first time. Some are used by stage magicians even today; others have strategic and tactical considerations. Some are pure fantasy. That is also a part of what must be learned—that the historical martial trilogy of mind, body and spirit, like so many other things in the world, are merely symbols, code words for simple, basic ideas, crammed and distorted by a classical mess.

Mind is memory, spirit is imagination, and body is touch, the test of reality created by mind and spirit. Hallucinations can be seen, but not touched. Voices may be heard, but not touched. Tangible, repeatable, empirical experimental evidence is the only test of reality on this plane.

Remember, also, that the human being is possessed of an automatic defense mechanism known clinically as the fight-or-flight adrenalin response. This is also seen in Nature and is a well-documented fact. As of this moment, we shall begin to associate this physio-chemical phenomenon, which endows the body with tremendous strength, heightened awareness, and lightning reflexes, toward the task of becoming invisible. In so doing we assume conscious control of the defensive aspect of this response and program it with a type of behavior which has been proven through the centuries to be highly effective.

The "adrenal pump" is activated by fear, and when one experiments with fear, one must be prepared for the consequences. The "dark side" of the Self is always ready to engulf those who would use such power for personal gain or self-aggrandizement, but it is only by making the inner journey, bathing in the pool of the subconscious and gazing into the mirrored, reflected image or this "dark self" or "shadow," that true understanding is possible. Therefore, do not step lightly upon the Moonlit Path of the Silent Way, for it will change your life. It is the road to self-knowledge, and through that, knowledge of others. It is an Inner Vision Quest. It is a puzzle, wrapped in a mystery, surrounded by an enigma of our own creation. But it can be done, and is well worth the effort.

1

THE BOOK OF EARTH

"The Grain of Sand in the Eye"

"Grain of sand in eye can hide mountain."
—Sidney Toler
(playing Charlie Chan), 1937

The first duty of any martial art worth its salt is to provide its students with an adequate means of self-defense. Most schools spend years helping their students develop the skills and moral outlook necessary for real competence in fighting. Here is a simple and effective technique that can be used by anyone, with no practice whatsoever.

Probably the most ancient technique for disabling an enemy is by blinding him, temporarily or permanently. Perhaps the tactic that best serves to illustrate this point is the art of throwing dirt in the eyes of an opponent. In motion pictures, this is sometimes done by the villain and is considered to be an unfair or dirty trick—but what is more unfair than being beaten to death?

In fact, this method probably developed when a smaller

11

adversary was thrown to the ground by a larger one and found his hands full of earth as a natural course of events. Hurling this virtually weightless substance at an onrushing foe might well have been a reflex, unlikely to have any effect. Still, who can deflect a handful of sand? At the very least, the attacker will blink instinctively, and therefore provide the opportunity for the defender to escape.

This is where the Art of Invisibility begins.

Far from being futile, such a defense is the single most effective nonviolent method of disappearing yet devised. Depending on the composition of the powder or dust used to blind an attacker, injury may be anything from momentary discomfort to permanent blindness.

BLACK EGGS

The ancient Ninja of the Black Dragon School carried their blinding powders in specially constructed containers, ready for instant use. These were called *hai lan,* or "black eggs." They were made by poking a small hole in both ends of an egg and then blowing into the shell so that the contents are forced out the other end. In this way the raw egg can be extracted without breaking the shell. The egg will now be very fragile, so be careful.

With a razor or sharp knife, open one of the blowholes a bit more widely, or cut the eggshell in half so it may be filled with the blinding powder. Let the shell dry completely.

Fill the eggshell with your secret formula, each *ryu* (school) has its own. This may be the ash of a particular tree indigenous to the tribal area of the clan, finely ground bone chips, salt, dry bleach, beach sand, or any similar material. Exotic compounds include certain weeds and alkaloid plants that produce a sparkling effect when reacting with the water from tears. Various peppers can produce temporary blindness; even the filings from a sharpened sword could be included to scratch the cornea and thereby inflict more permanent damage.

Seal the eggshell back together with glue. The Ninja of old had several formulas for this, but today commercially available adhesives are more than adequate. Once dry, the eggshell becomes a perfect container for a handful of dust and is easily hidden in the hand. It is too fragile to carry in a pocket, but because of its fragility, it will easily spill its contents just when you need it to.

Harden the eggshell by painting it with several thick coats of lacquer or black paint. A little bit of experimentation will determine how much is needed. You are now armed with one of the most ancient and secret of all Ninja weapons—*Hai Lan.*

SHADOW DUST

At this juncture, a special word should be said about the practice of "hiding in the shadows." While this may seem to belong more properly to the category of camouflage, it is also part of the manufacture of black eggs, or Ninja dust bombs.

The Ninja discovered that the lighter the material that composed the contents of these eggs, the longer it was likely to hang in the air and be an effective barrier to vision. Some experimentation proved that ashes and dust were the best simple powder for this purpose. Being frugal and not wishing to waste anything, the humble Ninja did not throw away the ashes from his fire, any more than he discarded the contents of the egg. He ate the egg to give him strength and turned the shell into a weapon. Likewise, in his housecleaning, scuttling about his dwelling, or busily sweeping as a servant to some lord, the Ninja was also collecting ammunition for his blinding device. Since dust was often found in corners, under stairs, and above doorways one engaged in cleaning would naturally become familiar with those places and so be better able to conceal himself in their shadows, should the need arise. Also, when watching an enemy in preparation for an ambush, collecting and sifting dust or sand serves to calm the mind by giving the hands something to do.

Thus, hiding in the shadows is more than just a technique of Inpo (the art of breaking in or hiding); it is also a meditation on stillness and silence, and part of the practice for later skills that involve collecting and cultivating Qi, the life force which surrounds and pervades all things.

THE CLOUD OF DUST

Two methods of delivering the Ninja dust bomb against an opponent present themselves automatically. One is to crush the egg in the hand and throw the contents into the enemy's face using any one of a great variety of flinging methods, many of which are seen in the art of *Shuriken-Jitsu*, named for the star-shaped multipointed blades for which Ninja are famous. Range, of course, is limited, owing to the lightness of the tiny particulate missiles involved. The practice for this technique is to throw a dry washcloth at a head-sized target. This will fly about as well and as far as a handful of dust, and so provides good training and evaluation for the student without making a mess.

The second method is to crush the egg, exposing the contents, turn the open palm up in front of the lips and blow the powder into the face of the opponent. Obviously, this is a closer-range technique, but with some practice one can propel the dust a yard or more.

The third method is the basis of the myth that Ninja had grenades that exploded on impact and created a cloud of smoke in which they would vanish. Given the crude gunpowder of the era and the natural aversion to carrying something that might blow up in your pocket should you fall on it, the Ninja practiced throwing the dust bombs *against the ceiling* so that the powder would rain down, forming a curtain behind which they might vanish. To the untrained eye, this has the appearance of throwing something on the floor and having it explode upward.

Like many things that first seem amazing, when the explanation is known, they are quite simple. That is what makes it "magic."

This technique, Blowing Powder in the Enemy's Face, was used with great efficacy in the motion picture *The Serpent and the Rainbow* (1979). The subject dealt with Haitian voodoo and was based on the true adventure of a modern scientist researching the subject. The dust was a hallucinogenic mixed with a small amount of puffer fish poison, which conducted the psychedelic directly through the skin of the victim.

Blowing powder in the enemy's face (A)

Blowing Powder in the Enemy's Face (A)

Holding the powder-filled eggshell concealed in the hollow of the hand, move into effective range, which can be established with a little practice. Crush the eggshell in the palm. The noise will attract the enemy's attention; it is one that is recognizable but unusual in combat. Thus, he hesitates to see where it came from. Watch his eyes. When he blinks or looks at your hand, he has lost the battle.

Blowing Powder in the Enemy's Face (B)

Immediately turn the palm up, in the manner of a magician showing you a treasure he has just produced. In the voodoo method, the "assassin" would walk right up to the victim, smiling all the way—the "Poof!" After preparing for this moment by taking a lungful of air and then tightening the belly to charge, blow the dust off your open hand with a single forceful gust of wind, as when blowing out a stubborn candle. Aim for the eyes, intending the particles to elicit the involuntary blinking response of the human eye. This requires only two-hundredths of a second and cannot be stopped without years of practice in staring. Thus you temporarily blind him, and so become invisible. His blindness will last from five to forty-five seconds, depending on the magic powder used. In that amount of time you can walk away or get help.

Blowing Powder in the enemy's face (B)

ALL THAT GLITTERS...

Magicians and illusionists enhance the effect of blinding powders and make them less fearsome by using glitter dust. Symbolically, it is the same thing. You catch the eye of the audience or attacker and distract him from the real action.

This is the same sparkling, shredded bits of aluminum foil that most children in kindergarten learn to glue onto cardboard, paper, and each other. It makes a dazzling display.

These require no preparation after being purchased. The

tops of the little plastic tubes come off easily, enabling the user to scatter the spray of metallic color and reflection by simply tossing it upward. Being heavier than dust or ash, the particles will fall more quickly. Therefore, the hiding place to which you will flee, having been selected before trying this ploy, must be close at hand.

The single-hand toss is the most basic way of delivering the Ninja dust bomb, glitter dust, or any such powder weapon, as well as coins, sand, or a bowl of hot soup. Drop the lead hand, the one nearest the target, to waist level, holding the broken eggshell in a loose fist, to conceal it from the enemy.

Single hand toss

Single Hand Toss

Quickly toss the dust upward, opening your loose fist to spray the powder into the face of the adversary. Again, a little practice goes a long way. You can also toss the dust between you and the adversary to form a temporary screen that will hide you from view long enough to duck away. Alternatively, toss it up hard against the ceiling to make him look up at the noise and be showered with the dust.

Some ancient wizards added to the confusion of such a

display by leaving behind a talisman, magic sign, mouse, frog or bird. The victim of this trick unconsciously associates the living creature with the magician and mistakenly assumes that the sorcerer has turned himself into the animal. Furthermore, the familiar pet or beast attracts the attention of the victim, drawing his gaze away from you. This is the basis for the legend that vampires could turn into bats, that illusionists can turn into tigers, and that Ninja could likewise "morph" into some other life form.

When blown into the eyes, powdered jimsonweed, available throughout the southwestern United States, creates the same sparkling effect as glitter dust, but chemically instead of visually.

SIMPLE TREASURES

Today, the simplest way of applying the old sand-in-the-eye trick is to fill a small plastic bag with flour and loosely seal it with a bit of tape. The bag can be opened by lifting the flap and dumping the contents through the hole, by ripping it in half to create a large display in a single motion, or by cutting into the plastic with a finger or thumbnail and tearing a hole through which the powder may then be dispersed.

Another method of throwing a handful of sand, dust, or rocks into the face of the enemy is to toss the ruptured bag upward with both hands, as if scooping out water from a bucket.

Throwing Sand

In many emergency situations a handful of sand may be obtained by suddenly crouching down, as if fearful of being struck. After very little practice, you can launch the tiny missiles toward the enemy, either by using both hands at once, one hand at a time, or by cupping the hands together. All are equally effective in making the enemy look away so you can escape.

Throwing sand

THROWING TECHNIQUES

The method for practicing this technique is to cast the powder forcefully onto a wall or sheet so the various splatter patterns can be seen and the most effective chosen. With a minimal amount of effort, even the meek and mild can overcome the high and mighty.

It should be noted that much focus has been placed on the art of *Shuriken-Jitsu* (throwing stars or darts) with much emphasis on the implements themselves—how sharp they are, how much penetration is achieved, and so on. The masters of the true art, however, will tell you that the real secret of throwing is to be gentle. If the proper method of throwing is accomplished even a penny can be as deadly as an arrow. One should use the *tonki* (shuriken), stars, knives, or spikes to practice throwing accurately; then anything can be a weapon.

THE SQUEEZE BOTTLE

Another method of projecting powder into the eyes of an enemy is by means of the squeeze bottle. This can be easily constructed by emptying any of the many soft, plastic containers available on the market today, drying out the inside, and refilling it with a finely ground powder, such as talc.

The aperture, or nozzle, must be of sufficient width to permit passage of the particles when pressure is directed against the sides of the container. Furthermore, some sort of loose-fitting or easily removable cap must be in place to prevent accidental spillage. Something as simple as a small bit of wax placed over the end can be adequate; the wax will be blown off when the bottle is squeezed.

The squeeze bottle, like the poison water gun, increases the effective range of the weapon. It is customary to paint such devices black so they blend with the uniform, or flesh tone, and are not easily visible in the hand before use.

Squeeze-bottle projecting powder

Squeeze-Bottle Projecting Powder

Here the stream of powder is clearly seen and the effectiveness of this nonviolent weapon is clearly demonstrated. Virtually no movement is required to initiate this attack. Multiple dispersals can be employed, each of lesser volume and pressure as the contents run out.

The best place to carry such a contraption is on the wrist or forearm, one of the reasons why so many of the Ninja wore gauntlets. This permits ready access without the necessity of delving into pockets, which might alert an opponent. Another alternative is to attach a short string or cord to the bottle so it can hang from the wrist, ready to be captured by the palm and the contents expelled in a single motion. Of course, this requires a bit more practice than some of the other methods.

MOUTH MIST

At the time of this writing, there is a professional wrestler known only as Kendo Nagasaki, the "Black Ninja." I have seen him fight. He uses a trick known as the Earth-method Dragon Breath. At a crucial moment in many of his bouts, he emits from his mouth a green powder mist. Opponents struck in the face with this weapon immediately clutch their eyes and writhe on the mat in agony. While I have no way of knowing if the method to be presented here is the means whereby this gentleman performs his feat, it is, nonetheless, one way of dispersing a dry powder from the mouth.

Since bamboo is plentiful in Japan, it was only a matter of time before someone got the idea of using a pipe stem to propel darts and powders at the enemy. A small joint of bamboo, filled with powder and capped with wax on both ends, can be easily hidden in the mouth and used as indicated.

The reason it is called the Earth-method of the Dragon Breath Technique is because dry powder and sand are of the earth. They are the natural weapons the Ninja is given by the earth. There are many methods of tossing, throwing, or pro-pelling such missiles, and blowing them out of a tube is a function of the wind (Air), one of the Five Elements. The Dragon Breath Technique is properly classified as an Air element, but one can also spit water, as will be seen in the next section, or air, or dry powder, if one knows how.

KASUMI JUDO

Suppose, however, that you are caught without your secret weapon? How will you vanish then?

Not to worry—the Ninja have a technique for that unfortunate circumstance as well. It is called *Kasumi,* the mist or fog, and here is the earth-method for using it.

Kasumi (A)

Kasumi (A)

Stand at parade rest or ready stance, squarely facing the aggressor with hands clasped in back or front and knees slightly bent. In Kuji Kiri, the finger-knitting positions of Ninja meditation, the eighth position is one in which all the fingers are extended wide to symbolize the "control of the elements of Nature," a signal to others of the clan of awareness of the Five Elements. In a moment you will signal this, unarmed, to the aggressor, so that he cannot miss the message.

Kasumi (B)

As he steps forward to grab you, deflect his arm by raising both arms upward from the shoulder, bending the knees to lower the hips and head defensively, and aim the backs of your wrists at his face. Through depth perception, his eyes will see the ends of your arms and judge the danger presented as they come into range. They will seem quite far away, so most people will react slowly to the threat.

Kasumi (B)

Kasumi (C)

Kasumi (C)

Flick the fingertips of both hands upward into his face to make him blink by touching his eyelashes, which again elicits an involuntary response. Of course, that would be an ideal application. Barring that, any proximity of the fingertips to within two inches of the eyes is sufficient to cause the blink response. What he would see, if his eyes were open, would be both palms and outstretched fingers, and that would be all. He would not see that you had ducked down or bent your knees.

Kasumi (D)

Kasumi (D)

With your right leg, cross step in front and step behind the opponent by pivoting on the right heel, striking him in the chest or throat with your forearm while passing beneath his outstretched arm. This jars the chest or phrenic nerve in the neck, which operates the diaphragm. Injury causes it to slow down so he cannot breathe.

Kasumi (E)

Swing behind him with your left leg and wrap your left arm around his throat to choke him. Hold his head in place while

Kasumi (E)

you press your fist against the base of his skull. Hold your right bicep in your left hand to form a figure-4 lock around his neck. This is a secure hold from Greco-Roman wrestling. The pressure produces temporary blindness through trauma to the primary cerebral cortex of the brain, which controls all vision; cut off the blood supply and darkness envelops the victim. After pressure is released, impaired vision will last as long as when pressure was applied to produce the effect.

This is also the position for the Japanese Sleeper Hold, performed by using the right palm to push the head forward so that the throat is pressed into the V of the left elbow, cutting off the flow of blood to the head by constricting the carotid arteries on both sides of the neck.

When your enemy passes out, you become invisible.

This vanishing technique is the first to be learned because Earth is the first of the elements. It may be used with any of the blinding methods given or yet to come. It is a Wood method from "The Book of Earth," because it is a technique which employs "spiral" action.

There are three types of motion: linear, circular, and spiral, the last being a combination of the first two. Among the Five

Elements, Earth is a linear or Yang element, as is Fire. The epitome of all techniques—for both linear and circular have their applications—is a combination of the two.

The linear part of the technique is the "handflash" in the face. Lift straight up, arms and fingers straight. The circular part is the cross-step behind the opponent. Wood is used to symbolize spiral motion because it represents circular motion around a linear axis, the very pattern of the Universe itself.

It is useful to combine the Kasumi Judo trick with a loudly shouted command to startle the opponent and make it easier to flick your fingers in his face. In martial arts, this is called a *Kiai*, or spirit shout. It also tightens the belly to stir courage. Development of this technique is a product of meditation, and is the test at the end of each book.

KINDLING THE INNER FIRE

Let's say you have managed to "disappear." What will you do now? Well, usually you must hide. That requires patience, so the Ninja developed the Exercise of Stillness: how to sit and breathe quietly while waiting for pursuit to end. To pass the time, they practiced Kuji Kiri, the Japanese version of Qi Gong, or breathing exercises, to calm the mind and heal the body.

The Body is the vessel that holds the spirit. That is why it represents the Earth element.

The Breath is the spirit. Many cultures believe that an infant is not alive until it takes its first breath. At that time, the spirit enters the body, bringing with it all the knowledge required to exist in an air environment instead of a water one.

The Mind is the will, which binds them together.

Before one can learn to be a "fire-breathing dragon," one must first learn about Fire and Breathing. To accomplish this, the ancients have provided a series of exercises which act on both the conscious and subconscious levels. They must be learned in the proper sequence given on the fingers, each level building on the one below it. Do not leap ahead, lest injury result.

The first step is to draw air into the vessel, then to extract from it the essence required to sustain the body. Just as the digestive system extracts nutrients from food, the lungs extract oxygen from the air.

The Greeks called the vital force of the air *pneuma*. The Hindus refer to it as *prana*. The Chinese call it *qi*, the Japanese, *ki*. By whatever name, it is not only the molecules of nitrogen, hydrogen, and oxygen that make up our air, but also the electrical potential that holds the atoms together. When gases change from oxygen to carbon dioxide, a finite amount of energy is released, evident, and observable. Accept for a moment the principle of modern physics that energy cannot be destroyed, then that energy went somewhere. It is found in the chakras, or energy wheels, of the body, playing on the surface of the skin in the acupuncture channels and aura; it is the force of life. It is exactly this type of chemical reaction that releases energy to muscles to make the fibers contract and the body move. On a molecular level, adenosine diphosphate is transformed into adenosine triphosphate to power the muscles. This is a medical fact known as the Krebs cycle.

So the goal of this first exercise is to extract from the air both the gases needed to maintain life and the Qi ("chee"), the force which is everywhere, filling, penetrating, and surrounding all things. In the martial arts this is used to harden the body and make it invulnerable to spear, sword, arrow, serpent's fang, and tiger's claw.

The cultivation of the force is meditation.

Kuji Kuri (A)

Sit in the Half Lotus Posture, or Adept's Pose. The right leg is folded beneath the body to sit on the heel. The left leg is folded with the left foot resting on the right thigh.

Kuji Kuri (B)

Touching the middle fingertips to the thumbs connects the psychic channels in the arms. This is the first of the mudra, or finger-knitting positions, of Kuji Kiri.

Kuji Kuri (A) and (B)

Inhale slowly and deeply through the nose, filling the lungs from bottom to top, like pouring water into a glass. This is the first breathing exercise of Kuji Kiri; it is called deep breathing. Most people only use the upper third of their lungs for respiration.

Draw the air deep into the Tan T'ien, the One-Point two inches below the navel, the center of gravity and balance of the physical body, the Golden Stove in Chinese medicine. This is called "kindling the fire." Note that the lower belly expands as you breathe in and contracts as you breathe out, and that this is the same lower belly that we have said many times should be tightened, just as one charges the enemy in combat. Symbolically, the Golden Stove will "cook" the Juice of Jade, described in the "Book of Water," until the "steam" rises to the Mysterious Chamber, the head.

Exhale slowly and completely through the mouth by gently compressing the lower belly, expelling all impurities and negative emotions from the body. This is the first relaxation exercise. It is called "sighing," a natural and instinctive stress-relieving technique known to all.

The first form to be studied is called natural breathing. Most people breathe with their lungs, usually with the upper chest alone. To do so is to limit the amount of lung area available for oxygen exchange. The ancients have taught us to "breathe with the belly": inhale fully and deeply, letting the lower abdomen, below the belt, expand as if filling with air. This opens the lower lungs so more oxygen can permeate the blood. Then let the belly deflate as the exhalation is made. One should repeat this for at least twenty minutes at the beginning and end of any meditation. For a beginner, however, three of four are enough to start with, lest you hyperventilate.

This exercise will calm the mind, heal the body, and improve the digestion. It is sometimes helpful to visualize clean, pure air coming into the body and impurities or negative emotions being gently expelled, and to listen to the sound of respiration and gradually make it slow, soft, and silent so it cannot be heard even by yourself. Then you can hide effectively.

You might want to mentally or verbally repeat some positive affirmation. A short phrase, such as "In comes the good air, out goes the bad" can be very effective. At the conclusion of each session you will be relaxed and refreshed.

What has all this to do with becoming or staying invisible, you may ask. Suppose you are confronted by a bully who takes hold of your shirt to prevent your escape, and you haven't had time to steal your black egg from its secret pocket. Not to worry— you are now armed with Qi, what martial artists call inner strength.

For them, Qi is drawn into the Tan T'ien, below the belt, compressed, and directed to the fist, forging it into a deadly weapon; or it is channeled to some other part of the body to make it impervious to injury or to heal a wound; or, in the case of the Ninja Fire-Breathing Dragon Technique, it is used to propel a fireball at a target. This is the first step in developing the technique. It cannot be omitted.

THE USES OF FEAR

When one is frightened, the rate of respiration changes, contributing to and caused by fear. Natural breathing calms this anxiety, and that alone is reason enough to practice it. Now, however, we shall apply it to the art of self-defense.

As fear grows, you feel the "bottom drop out of your stomach," because your adrenal glands have been activated by the "fight-or-flight" response, another involuntary reflex common to all humans. When this happens, take a deep breath. Draw air deep into the belly, filling and expanding it in the same manner as when meditating. This will calm the adrenal effect and give you control over your reaction, enabling you to perceive the situation clearly and react spontaneously. Exhale about 10 percent and tighten the belly; this helps prevent injury and screws up courage. The samurai had a saying, "When afraid, tighten the belly and charge!"

Look the attacker "dead in the eyes" by focusing on his forehead. This is a very subtle trick used by magicians and hypnotists. It makes the subject feel inferior, and can be used to intimidate those of lesser will. Fix his attention on your eyes as you inhale. This is a psychological response to his challenge. By engaging his vision, you accept and signal to him with you body language that you are preparing to fight. This will make him hesitate. It may even make him release you, preventing further escalation of violence.

If this fails, then, as you finish inhaling and tighten the lower belly, blow forcefully into the face of the attacker. Don't try to "blow out all the candles" in one breath and empty yourself. Save some air with which to strike a blow or run away. Even a short blast will make him blink.

PRACTICING BREATH CONTROL

Blowing Out a Candle

Here is a practice method for developing this technique. Stand poised in a firm Horse Stance at arm's length from the

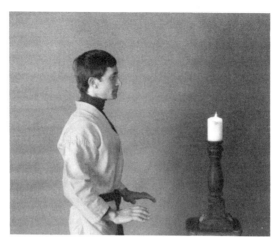

Blowing out a candle

candle. Concentrate on the flame as you breathe in. Without moving closer, practice blowing out the candle by exhaling short puffs of air from the belly. Correct your aim by blowing a steady stream of air and watching for the flame to flicker.

This is the test of Qi Gong, breath control. When you can put out the candle with a single puff at arm's length, you will have learned the technique. There is no way the enemy can block it or prevent himself from blinking. At that instant, MOVE!

Decide whether to jerk away from his grasp or seize him in a painful wristlock while inhaling, but don't be indecisive—it will be fatal.

Advanced practice for this technique is to put the candle at eye level. Begin by blowing gently until you can see the effects of your breath on the flame. You should be able to make it move back and forth as you inhale and exhale from about three feet away. When you can do that, bend it toward you and away by will alone. Do this for a while, then blow it out in a single puff. Gradually move farther back until you can snuff it out from about three feet away. Blowing out a candle at eye level is quite different from blowing down onto a table.

Do not strain. Do not sputter. Do not try to go beyond arm's

length. The technique can be done from greater distances, but
then one tends to whistle or spit.

STONE DRAGON

A Shaolin teaching declares, "The Earth Dragon is made of
stone. Rooted to the ground, it cannot be moved." Stone
Dragon (Earth) techniques include linear punches and kicks,
takedowns, breakdowns, and throws to get the enemy on the
ground, where the aggressor can be finished with mat-work.
Anatomy, the understanding of the body, the earthly manifestation of the spirit, is learned, just like the vital and fatal points,
as demonstrated by the fist-to-base-of-skull technique, which
can also be used to heal. Stone Dragon is only a small part of
the Ninja Iron Body system, which enables the user to endure
hardship and withstand pain.

The classic Dragon's Head Fist of some styles of Kung Fu is
known in Ninjitsu as the Shoulder Punch, in which the fingers
are curled into the palm and the thumb is folded over to lock
them in place. This hardens the fist and exposes the two
foremost knuckles of the index and middle fingers as the
striking surface.

Punching Out a Candle (A)

The fist is "loaded," palm up, on the hip. Place the candle at
the level of the solar plexus. Stand in a firm Horse Stance. Extend
the other hand edge up, as shown, or palm forward to simulate
an attempt to ward off an attacker. This is to establish the range
that enables the Ninja to find and strike his opponent, even in
total darkness, by using the sense of touch. The target is the
xyphoid process on the tip of the sternum. If this is struck with
as little as eight pounds of pressure, the diaphragm will cease
pumping and the victim will fall to the floor. No permanent
injury will result unless he is struck harder. You may never strike
an attacker like this, but you do need to develop hand speed and
concentration for some of the later techniques.

Punching out a candle (A)

Punching Out a Candle (B)

Throw the punch from the hip, twisting the fist over at the last second to "snap" the punch, stopping just short of the flame. The aim is to use air compressed in front of the fist to snuff out the flame without it actually being struck. When you can "punch out" a candle in this manner, you can knock out the

Punching out a candle (B)

average man with one punch. The left arm is snapped back to the left hip as the fist strikes to counterbalance the movement and add to its impact.

Note that this is a linear punch. Compare it to the (circular) Hidden Hand Technique in "The Book of Water."

2

THE BOOK OF WATER

"The Pool of the Subconscious"

"The Water Dragon resides in the Pool of the Subconscious Mind."
—Shaolin teaching

Its weapons are poison spray, like that used in the Ninja poison water gun, two interlocking tubes that, when compressed, eject a stream of toxic liquid toward an attacker. There is also the more modern liquid tear gas, as well as self-defense sprays, like a water pistol of ammonia. Another weapon is breath control, as demonstrated by the ability to remain submerged for long periods. Finally, there is the understanding of the Five Emotions and Five Desires. This is the level of the subconscious mind where a near dreamlike state may be induced through autosuggestion to produce long-lasting results in a short period of time.

SPIT IN THE EYE

With all the previous discussion about Tan T'ien and expelling puffs of air from the lungs, one might wonder, Why not proceed with the next logical step, that of spitting in the eye of the enemy?

This has long been regarded as a heroic if somewhat futile gesture in the face of certain doom. It would seem to be more of an insult or an act of defiance than an attack. It may be that this was how this act was first intended, but if performed at the right time and followed by one of the vanishing steps, it is clearly useful as a means of attaining invisibility.

Spitting, therefore, is an example of a vanishing technique representing the Water element. Like the previous element, Earth, it is known as the Water-method Dragon Breath. Once aware of this technique, the wise martial artist is never un-armed. One Kung Fu expert bragged in a recently published martial arts magazine that he could spit accurately up to ten feet. Accuracy is key.

It is not called in-the-eye for nothing: The eye is the best target. In fact, it is the only target worthy of a drop of water.

There are various ways to attempt this. Individual experi-mentation is the best way of discovering the most suitable method. Bear in mind that this is a weapon and not just random rudeness. Don't aim at the ground. Spitting on someone's boots is an insult, and almost certain to draw a response, but it is not a self-defense move.

Don't "overload" either. Due to the sensitive nature of the eye and the blink reflex, which, it will be recalled, even responds to wind, a small amount of water is more than sufficient and easier to generate and propel with any degree of accuracy. When you can project at eye level for about eighteen inches, return to the candle and practice spitting it out. Over time, move the target farther and farther away until you have found the natural limit of your range. This should be about arm's length, and represents the limits of one's sphere of influence, or "personal space."

As the aggressor prepares to attack, accumulate a mouthful of saliva, or, if a drink is handy, conceal a sip of the liquid by not swallowing it. Return the stare of the adversary steadily. Being "armed," a defender has an edge and so can act with confidence in the face of danger. Not speaking back against his verbal abuse will also confuse him. (Of course, you can't speak because you have a mouthful of liquid.) Thus, the technique produces the body language signals that may, by themselves, halt him.

Before he can launch his attack, or at the moment when he makes his verbal challenge and demands an answer, spew the liquid in his face and eyes. This will blind him for an instant, with no permanent injury. Be sure to be out of sight by the time he wipes his eyes and regains his vision, since it will almost certainly make him angry, and his ego, which brought him to this challenge in the first place, will demand revenge.

THE JUICE OF JADE

To demonstrate the degree of detail into which the Ninja delved in order to augment their techniques, we present an exercise known in ancient times as Red Dragon Washes the Waves. It can be done in a seated, meditation position, therefore qualifying as an "internal" exercise, one which circulates the life force, Qi Gong. It is, or was, designed as a method of brushing the teeth long before the invention of the toothbrush—by the Chinese, incidentally. (Since they recognized that good digestion was largely dependent on proper chewing or mastication of food into nutrients, good dental hygiene became a hallmark of their medical practice.)

Sitting in a comfortable, cross-legged pose with eyes closed, back straight, and head up, lightly run the tip of your tongue around the inside of your teeth from left to right (clockwise) eighteen times, then from right to left (counterclockwise), eighteen times. Swish the generated saliva back and forth in the mouth thirty-six times and divide it into three portions. Swallow each with a gulp into the lower belly. This exercise stimulates and massages the teeth and gums, removes plaque, and prevents tooth decay. It is also an excellent method of producing spittle with which to practice self-defense. "Brush" twice a day.

The Chinese believe that the saliva is charged with positive and negative ions through the manipulations of the Red Dragon (tongue), which is the reason for the equal number of rotations in each direction. One should also observe that when the numbers are totaled (18 + 18 + 36), the sum is seventy-two, whose digits add up to nine, the prime number of *Shugendo,* the Yamabushi sect of Buddhism associated with Japanese Ninjitsu. In Chinese medicine, nine is a Yang, or positive number, while six is Yin.

The Chinese call this charged saliva the Juice of Jade and believe that it calms the mind, heals the body, and improves digestion. Certainly, the increase in digestive enzymes alone must have some beneficial effect, but, beyond this, the three portions swallowed represent Heaven, Earth, and Man, the three levels of being. Thus, a certain degree of philosophy is also included, and martial artists know this method as "uniting mind, body, and spirit." Therefore, it is not wise to waste too much of this precious fluid in mere candle extinguishing just so you know you can generate a weapon, if need be.

SPEWING WATER

Having accomplished the first exercise, let us turn now to the simplification method. Instead of using personal body fluids to practice spitting, employ a small cup of water and practice spewing sips and later streams of liquid at the flame. Try to eventually learn to spray the liquid to form the "mist" or "fog" alluded to in the Earth method.

Do not sputter, but strive to have the water clear your lips completely, using pressure of the lungs and lower belly to expel the smaller amounts in a single jet of spray, and the big mouthfuls in a continuous stream. Do not run out of air before you run out of liquid!

It is possible to see that any liquid could be used in a similar manner. A cup of coffee becomes a lethal weapon against more than one attacker by spraying a sip on the leader and throwing the rest at a second enemy so that a quick strike can be made and an escape effected. Even Chinese tea, or hot soup, can be thrown like a Ninja dust bomb with the same effect. All symbolize Water.

TOBACCO JUICE

Obvious extensions of this technique include the use of tobacco juice. The somewhat disreputable habit of chewing tobacco does have a self-defense function, if one chooses to cultivate it. The reason for bringing it up is more to make one aware of the possibility of such a defense, than to advocate its practice. One of the greatest American cult heroes, Clint Eastwood, used this device in the film *The Outlaw–Josie Wales* (1976) in a classic example of using a "bad" means to achieve a worthwhile goal. Nicotine poisoning of the eyes will induce great discomfort and temporary blindness. A certain caustic effect should be anticipated, but not sufficient to cause scarring. Furthermore, the pungent aroma assaults the nostrils of the victim in a manner similar to the Dragon Breath Technique, given in the fourth book, Air. It also results in the mental discomfort from being spat on, stained, and embarrassed.

ACID BREATH

Further discussion of techniques for projecting noxious liquids from the mouth must include some mention of the odd one used by still another oriental wrestler of the professional arena, Killer Khan, who claims to be from Mongolia and performs the salt scattering ceremony of the Sumo ring before each of his matches.

Like the Black Ninja, Khan can at the critical moment spew into the face of his hapless opponents a green liquid that stains the face and causes such pain that they are compelled to clutch their fists to their eyes to relieve it. During this period of incapacity, they are invariably pinned by the almost-three hundred-pound Mongolian.

In Ninjitsu, this is known as Acid Breath, or Water-method Dragon Breath, and is performed as follows: Hold in the hollow chambers of the mouth until ready for use a chalklike tablet covered in wax to prevent it from dissolving prematurely; when ready, bite into the tablet, filling the mouth with a substance that produces and abundance of saliva as in the Juice of Jade exercise, only quicker and with less concentration. Simultaneously add the desired pigment to the mixture. The formula should not be too caustic, lest it burn the lining of the mouth and do more harm to the user than to the victim.

An example of this type of article is the frothing blood capsules sold around Halloween to simulate the blood from vampire fangs. When chewed or broken open, they produce a bright red tint and stimulate saliva production. Food coloring, however, works just as well, as the degree of salivation depends precisely on the amount of saliva required to digest the substance. A small cellophane pack of water-based paint hidden under the tongue will work too. When bitten open, the paint is not toxic enough to cause lasting discomfort, but it is distasteful enough to cause profuse salivation. Likewise, if one's bamboo self-contained blinding powder blowgun were to be accidentally opened, it might produce this same effect.

The exact method used by the wrestler in question is unknown, but it must necessarily be based on one or more of these same principles. It is most certainly of Far Eastern origin and founded on the principles of Chinese medicine, which holds the breath of the liver to be green. Interestingly, the gall bladder in the liver controls the bile, which is green and yellow, and bile is a symbol of anger. Bile is stimulated by that emotion. Without modern scientific methods, or having taken the inner journey of meditation, how could the ancients have known these things?

THE ART OF REGURGITATION

Of course, no discussion would be complete without raising the spectre of an even more distasteful and revolting sort of halatoctic attack, projectile vomiting. This technique is born of great mental distress and, without a doubt, life-and-death situations are stressful. Everyone gets "butterflies" in their stomach before they step onstage. This is a manifestation of the reflex required to master the rather obscure and relatively unknown art of voluntary vomiting.

Harry Houdini is said to have learned this trick from an old Chinese man while working in carnivals and dime museums. He used it to hide his tools and lockpicks from even the most stringent search. The training method is to tie a small round bit of potato to a string and endeavor to swallow it far enough down the esophagus to make it invisible, then retrieve it by using retro-peristalsis, the reverse of the muscle contractions that constitute swallowing. If lost, the potato and string would be digested. The purpose of the string is to pull the potato back up the throat the first few times, so it won't be swallowed, until you get the knack of regurgitating at will and not from too deeply in the stomach. This technique enables one to overcome the gag reflex.

The next step is to practice with an egg—a *hai lan*, black egg, perhaps? Again no problem to digest if lost, but don't eat too many at once. It is also possible to perform this feat without prior training, merely by being sufficiently terrified. Recruits do it in basic training in a fear response to verbal intimidation.

Like many legends about Harry Houdini, this one may or may not be true, but the method certainly sounds as if it would work. It is yet another example of a technique that trains the Ninja to have conscious control over many autonomic reflexes. One must first control the body, then the mind, and then the spirit will soar.

As before, one must consider these things in order to understand that there is always a way to achieve a goal, no matter how strange or improbable it may be.

POISON WATER GUN

For the more conservative, other methods include the Ninja poison water gun, counterpart to the Squeeze Bottle Technique of the "Book of Earth." It is a device much like a syringe, probably first made from two interlocking joints of bamboo, with a hole or venturi in the smaller end. When filled with marsh water, oil, or a similar liquid and pushed together, the increased pressure within the tubes propels a spray or stream at or onto an enemy.

In the modern era, a favorite weapon of spies is a glass syringe filled with prussic acid. When this is discharged into an enemy's face, it produces a gas that is instantly fatal. This weapon is much more easily concealed than a gun.

The famous, or infamous, bank robber Willie Sutton once broke out of prison due in part to his ability to overcome the guards by spraying chlorine in their eyes. He did this by raiding bleach from the laundry room and dispensing it from tennis balls with a slit in one of the sides. Just think what he might have accomplished with a water pistol. Even that simple toy, when filled with ammonia, will drive off a vicious dog. So, why not a mugger?

HIDDEN HAND

Water, it will be recalled, is a circular element, just as Earth is linear. Therefore, it is only logical that a martial art based on these principles should have a representative punch or fist, as the others do. We therefore come to the first circular technique of Ninja Invisible Fist system. It is called the Hidden Hand.

When one suffers from anoxia, as produced by the Sleeper-hold previously given, lack of oxygen to the brain produces disorientation, confusion, and often sparkling spots before the eyes. Many of the Judoka (practitioners of judo) report that the Japanese Strangle compels the victim to see a purple haze just before passing out. This is due to the eye's reaction to the brain shutting down, and is one of the last perceptions preceding loss of consciousness.

Earlier, we spoke of throwing glitter in the face of an attacker to use as a blinding powder, and now we mention the spots before an attacker's eyes just before the purple haze sets in. From the martial arts we now present a method of producing this effect with only one finger, in fact, with only one knuckle!

Fold the fingers into a firm fist, but extend the knuckle of the middle finger. Squeeze the other fingers under it together for support. Rap on a tabletop or other wooden surface as if knocking on a door. This hand formation is called the Buffalo Knuckle Fist, and is used to "knock" on someone's forehead.

Between and slightly above the eyes is the spot known as the Third Eye. It represents a meeting point for many important nerves and lies directly in front of the central sulci of the frontal lobes of the brain. A sharp blow to this point with the Phoenix Eye Fist, as this technique is also known, will disrupt the flow of nerve impulses from the eyes to the brain—not because great damage has been done to the skull, although it is possible for a trained martial artist to fracture the bones of the skull or break them; nor because it injures some psychic center of the brain, even though this is also true. Rather, the eyes are impaired because the brain will react to pain in the forehead, albeit minor, before it will answer signals from the eyes.

Such a blow will make the victim see "spots" before his eyes, which may turn inward or roll up into his head, indicating unconsciousness. A large red spot may appear at the site of the injury and may swell into a lump that can be reduced by applying ice. Almost every time, the victim will bring his palm to his forehead, effectively blinding himself by using his own hand to cover his eyes.

To produce the purple haze, strike straight against the Third Eye, as opposed to downward, as in the rapping technique. By traumatizing the nerves, the muscles of the eye relax, dilate, and roll out of focus for three to five minutes.

Inducing the purple haze (A) and (B)

Inducing the Purple Haze (A)

Form the Buffalo Knuckle by extending your middle joint of the middle finger above your fist. Form the Hidden Hand by covering your right fist with your left hand. This prevents the enemy from seeing that you have formed a hand weapon.

Inducing the Purple Haze (B)

Aim your left shoulder at your opponent to present a smaller target and hide your fist from view. Bend your knees slightly in anticipation of having to duck out of sight quickly, and lower your Tan Tien, or center of balance. Look over your left shoulder and fix your opponent's gaze by looking at his Third Eye. In the "knocking on the forehead" method, the fist makes a circle upward, across the chest, above the eyes and down onto the forehead after the hand-flash is executed. Both are circular motions representative of the enveloping nature of Water.

The Hidden Hand is the first technique of the Invisible Fist Sea Dragon (Water) Method. It can be learned quickly and easily by anyone and is almost instinctive when trying to fend off an attacker. For this reason, a large number of people can be trained in its use in a short period of time, making it possible for the Ninja to raise and train an army virtually overnight.

Inducing the purple haze (C) and (D)

Inducing the Purple Haze (C)

As the opponent advances intending to seize your uniform or shoulder with his leading hand, meet him halfway by taking a short step forward, lower your head, and close with him. Sweep his arm aside by swinging your left palm toward his face up and outward in a large circular arc from the previous on-guard stance. At the same time, swing your right fist out and back in a wide arc to gather momentum for the punch. If executing the "knocking" technique, let the fist swing up and over to strike downward on his forehead. The big trick here is the hand-flash before his eyes, which may be just as effective if he never lifts a finger. This is in keeping with the principle of "invisibility first," of the Ninja tradition.

Inducing the Purple Haze (D)

Or, swing the Buffalo Knuckle in a wide arc horizontally and strike the attacker in the left temple, as shown. This is a stunning blow, much more likely to produce unconsciousness or swelling, black eyes, and even broken bones, since the bones of the temporal region are much thinner than those of the forehead. It produces shocking pain in the head and numbing blindness for many minutes, but it is presented here because you may someday need to knock out an attacker who cannot be stopped any other way. This wild right-hook punch is also seen in boxing and is a valid technique. It comes over the leading shoulder of the opponent and has a lot of impact when the hips and shoulders are turned into the swing. Not only will your opponent see spots, he will be knocked out with one punch!

HARAKI

There is a branch of martial arts known and studied by only a few, called *haraki*. It is a Japanese word, composed of the ideograms for Hara, or the center of the physical body (Tan Tien), and Ki, the term for Qi, previously discussed and defined.

Haraki involves training oneself to draw in air, collect it and cultivate it in the center (inhaling breath), then transmit it with a shout, known in Karate the *kiai* or spirit-shout (exhaling breath). The effect is to tighten the belly so you can charge. It is a cry, scream, or yell, of total commitment, not at all like the mere grunts of so many other martial arts schools. The warrior puts all his strength and energy into one powerful finishing or deciding blow. It is a strong exhalation from the belly just as a strike is delivered. It is often seen and properly performed in *Tameshiwara,* or breaking demonstrations, where the student shatter bricks or boards with his bare hand. As indicated in "The Book of Earth," such a shout can be included in the execution of various vanishing or misdirection techniques.

In the martial arts, military training, and law enforcement, the value of a deep commanding voice is well recognized and documented, just as the hypnotic voice will be important to the material covered in "The Book of Air." Many a dispute has been settled by a firm tone and a steady timbre, and verbal orders in the field that drive young men into direct gunfire are the result of a programmed response initiated in basic training.

The relationship of this to water is that sound waves can be seen on water, making an invisible phenomenon visible. Thus, the Water element is associated with sound and sound waves.

The effectiveness in combat of the *kiai* is well proven: It can freeze an opponent in mid-step, startle him enough to make him jump out of his stance, or make him blink. The *kiai* is all that is required.

The range of the *kiai* is somewhat more extended than in the Blow in the Face technique, since the operating factor is sound rather than air. Some schools believe that all things are merely vibrating at different speeds. Solids are the slowest, then Liquids, then Air, Fire, and finally the most widely dispersed, the Void, symbolized by Wood. Within these are the vibrational planes of light and sound, each of which has a range above and below that which is perceptible to humans. Infrared rays are too long to be visible, but are so active that they break down chemical bonds. There exist sounds that are too low to be heard but which can be felt on the skin or through the whistles that only dogs hear.

Thus, sound is also a force that can be used as a weapon to temporarily blind an opponent.

REVERSE BREATHING

The meditation practice for *haraki* is known as Reverse Breathing. To perform this, let the belly contract as you inhale and expand as you exhale, the reverse of natural breathing. It is essential that these methods of breath control be practiced and learned well.

Again perform about twenty minutes of this in a relaxed and gentle manner. If one considers that natural breathing is a way of drawing in positive energy, or Qi, from the air, then it must follow that this energy is eventually transported to other parts of the body. This circulation occurs naturally, without conscious direction, otherwise life would not exist. With this practice, however, we begin to take conscious control of such autonomic reflexes so that mental direction of the energy is possible.

In a purely hydraulic way, such manipulations of the mental state will produce unconscious tension in certain parts of the body, and this will pump or shunt blood to other parts. In Yoga, sitting in the Full Lotus Pose soon puts the legs to sleep by restricting circulation, at least in the early stages. In so doing, however, blood is allowed to collect at the base of the spine. By tensing the belly, this excess can be pumped to the brain, "letting the steam rise" in Qi Gong. When coupled with the nervous impulses that must necessarily accompany such an event, and mental imagery that reinforces the process, one can stimulate the powers of the mind—or so it is said.

Even modern science admits that man uses only a small portion of his available brain cells and that a method of stimulating brain activity would be of benefit to mankind. By charging up the Qi from the air through hyperventilation in the first exercise, one has also oxygenated the bloodstream. In the Full Lotus Pose, a certain amount of this blood has accumulated at the base of the spine, ready for the sacral pump—pulling in the belly as you exhale to push blood to the brain.

In Reverse Breathing, this oxygen-rich blood floods over the brain, enriching and stimulating the entire organ. Unlike other parts of the body, the brain does not have an extensive system of capillaries to supply blood. Instead, it is essentially bathed in cerebro-spinal fluid while floating in the shallow brainpan. So the effect, for the user, is often like "lighting up the sky" or, as in the Zen texts, "the opening of the Thousand Petal Lotus."

Of course, such transcendental experiences cannot be adequately described, otherwise they would not be transcendental. Suffice to say, it is a unique experience that will make you feel better, think clearer, and be more alert, although completely relaxed, ready to meet whatever the day may offer.

THE HEAVENLY POOL

Now that the Fire has been kindled with natural breathing and the Qi refined in the Golden Stove, and the distillation of this is raised to the Mysterious Chamber by way of the Heavenly Pillar of the spine, all that remains is to let it condense and return to the Tan T'ien to complete the small Heavenly Cycle of Qi and begin the process of insuring peace of mind, good health, and longevity.

This is accomplished by touching the tip of the tongue to the roof of the mouth. The palate, tongue, teeth, and so on are known as the Heavenly Pool in Chinese medicine, where the Juice of Jade originated that was boiled to make the distilled vapor above. What is important, however, is that this chamber forms a gap in the energy channels of the body, only bridged by this exercise, to let the Qi circulate freely.

Shouting Out a Candle (A)

Practice "shouting out" the candle by assuming a Horse Stance at arm's length from the target. Inhale slowly and deeply, filling the lungs with air from bottom to top.

Shouting Out a Candle (B)

Exhale forcibly, from the belly, shouting a one-syllable command word, using the diaphragm to direct the sound at the

Shouting out a candle (A) and (B)

flame. Tighten the belly as you shout. Virtually any explosive sound can be used for the *kiai:* "Ha!" "Fish!" or even "Kiai!" A recognizable word may even be employed, such as "Stop!" "No!" or "Wait!" Any single syllable that is made by blowing outward can be used. "Om..." for example, is made by closing the lips and humming, which is why it is used for meditation rather than combat.

Shouting Out a Candle (C)

Practice *Haraki* by assuming a firm Horse Stance at arm's length from the candle. Clench the fists around the thumbs and set them on the hips. Concentrate the Qi and focus on the candle.

Shouting Out a Candle (D)

Without moving, exhale forcefully from the belly, making no sound. Direct the exhalation at the flame and extinguish it as before, this time using "silent" *kiai.* Compare the posture and

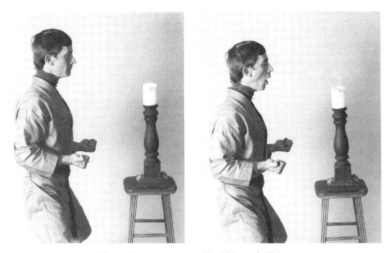

Shouting out a candle (C) and (D)

facial expression in this and the previous exercise. It will be seen that in the former, chest compression expels the air or sound. Here, it is a short, forceful compression of the belly.

3

THE BOOK OF FIRE

"The Fire-Breathing Dragon"

Thus far we have discussed two of the Five Elements, Earth and Water. The middle finger of the hand represents the Fire element. Within it flows the heart governor meridian of acupuncture and the Yang Yu psychic channel of the arm terminates at the tip of this digit, as well as many major nerves of the arm.

In this section we shall present the physical representation of the Fire element as it is taught to members of the Black Dragon Fighting Society who train in Ninjitsu. It has been described in many ways—as "savage and terrifying," as the "dark side" of martial arts, and other misnomers. All are part of the Ninja technique of Monami-no-Jitsu, which is translated to mean, "a head-dress seen from four sides, looks the same." In other words, a great deal of the world's misery is caused by misperception.

Sometimes the Ninja deliberately confuse the issue. There are many methods of presenting the oft-seen Yin-Yang symbol, for example, a circle, divided by an S-shape line, black on one side, white on the other, with a spot of the alternate colors of each side contained within the other. But there is only one way of presenting it in the primordial state; what would be considered the most ancient, most basic state.

Such fundamental techniques are, therefore, the most profound. Proof of this is their conformity to the established criteria.

In other presentations of Kata Dan'te (Dance of the Deadly Hands), great emphasis has been placed on performance of the twenty-seven movements, each one of which is capable of killing, crippling, or maiming any attacker, in ten seconds or less. The vital and fatal points of the body are so sensitive that they need not be struck with anywhere near the amount of force used in a ten-second burst of white-hot anger.

Some martial arts practitioners dismiss Kata—Japanese for "dance" and always spelled in the singular—as boring drills, unnecessary for the true fighter; or consider them the formal exercises of Karate, to be performed in robotic perfection to demonstrate to judges or teachers that they know all of the techniques required for advancement to the next level, i.e. more "belt rank"; or they may regard kata as the dance it was intended, like Capoiera, the Brazilian martial art whose disciples maintain a constant rhythmic step to confuse the enemy, much like a boxer would in the ring.

The Ninja know that all of these may be applied to any kata. In the last few years, tournaments have been besieged by students who insist on performing "kata to music." This makes a dramatic presentation, to be sure, but even that is limited, usually to one song.

The Ninja may perform Kata Dan'te in many ways, all depending on his mood or level of skill. The method that symbolizes the Fire element, however, is done much the same as a Tai Chi form. That is to say, very slowly and with very little force. In Tai Chi Chuan, it is said, "a force of one thousand pounds can be deflected by four ounces." Likewise here. This is the method whereby the acupuncture points that are considered targets for strong punches and powerful kicks in other systems, and even in the blinding speed practice method previously given, are merely pressed, or "touched." This is one method of employing Dim Mak, the Delayed Death Touch reserved only for masters of an art.

It is not necessary to inflict bodily harm or death on the attacker. The Ninja has absolute control of how much force is applied in any execution of these techniques against an attacker. You can have blood and gore if you must train quickly to strike hard, strike fast, and show no mercy. Or, you can practice the exact same movements slowly, concentrating on the vital or fatal acupuncture point to be "pressed"—a totally different approach than ripping flesh and breaking bones, which is only obtained through years of solo practice or direct transmission from teacher to student.

It should be noted that the other elements are also represented by kata. The Water form is smooth, flowing away and around the attacker. The Earth form (and there are several of each) always begins by taking a step backward, in retreat. The Air form, like water, flows, but this time diagonally forward instead of diagonally back and also encircles the attacker, like water. The Wood form takes no step, relying instead on leaping or crouching techniques and pivots—a "spiral" type of motion. These are the only Five Directions in which a human body can move, because there are only Five Elements.

While other descriptions of Kata Dan'te have referred to the various fists and hand strikes therein as being "dragon claw, tiger claw," and so on, the fact is that in the primeval Five Element Fist all of these were known as the Way of the Fire Hand. Just as some other styles have techniques they call the Wind Hand (International Taoist Society, London, England), the Ninja have five such categories. This is only one.

Later schools of Ninjitsu called it the Flaming Fist or Inferno Palm, and, as in the Iron Body methods used to train in Earth techniques, there is a practice method to "develop the fist." Incidently, one of the reasons this kata can truly be considered a Fire method is because, when done with blinding speed, the victim appears to have been incinerated or BBR, a NASA term for "burned beyond recognition."

When done as follows, however, it will be seen that the attacker is merely "put to sleep" by pressure against his vital and fatal points. A much gentler method but, because it acts against the nerve points, which in Chinese medicine are the symbol of Fire in the body, it still qualifies as a Fire element.

Hidden Hand

Hidden Hand

Kindling the Fire is the name used in Iron Body training to initiate the programmed series of movements (exercises) in the proper sequence to circulate Qi, or in this case, to stir the "fire of the will." The Ninja faces the attacker in the Hidden Hand Stance, seen previously to deliver the Buffalo Knuckle Strike.

Instead of presenting the left shoulder to the enemy as in that strike, here the Ninja makes a big target of himself in a psychological attempt to discourage an attack. Likewise, the Hidden Hand Stance itself is enough for most martial artists to recognize one highly skilled in the arts.

It is perfectly obvious that the Ninja, having long ago cooled his own anger through meditation, could just as easily defeat his adversary with a Water technique, without having to engage him in combat, because "water destroys fire," physically and psychologically, but in this instance, a conscious decision has been made to intervene, to "meet fire with fire," so to speak. The first step is to "psych up" for the fight, keeping the hot temper under control while "fanning the flames" of the enemy's anger. This is partly accomplished by standing calmly, waiting for him to make his move, as in the Hidden Hand Stance. The fist concealed by the left hand, in this case, is the Dragon Palm shown elsewhere in more detail. Bear in mind that in Chinese mythology, the dragon represents the Fire element.

Dragon Spreads Wings Block

The opponent launches his attack by taking a step forward and throwing a right hooking punch. The Ninja simultaneously performs three actions. The left foot takes a step forward, meeting the enemy's knee with your knee to block his step, and pushing down his foot to be pinned beneath your heel. On the instep is a large cluster of nerves that flow to the feet. Pressure on this point can be both painful and numbing. Likewise, banging the kneecap into the opponent's shin can produce a sharp, numbing pain for him.

Second, the Ninja swings his left arm up and outward as in the Buffalo Knuckle Strike to deflect the enemy's punch—except this time, the blow lands on the inside of the opponent's forearm instead of on the outside. As with the foot, striking the forearm of the enemy sharply with your forearm, as shown, or with the edge of the hand, can be used to numb the arm distally from the point of impact if the blow is directed against

Dragon Spreads Wings block

the radial nerve, which lies along the top of the forearm. In the blinding speed application, the intent is to break the enemy's arm. Here, it can be seen that striking the proper target with a small amount of force, usually only four pounds, the amount needed to break a 12 x 12-inch white pine board, often used as a "test of skill and power" in Karate schools, is sufficient to produce the desired effect. It is not necessary to "leap into the fray." A quick step is all that is required to close the distance to the opponent and "steal the march" from him. Further, by so doing, the Ninja places himself "inside the arc" of the punch, thereby lessening its momentum and potential impact.

Palm Heel to Chin

Palm Heel to Chin

Third of the three simultaneous actions is to place your forearm against the sternum of the opponent and slide your Palm Heel Fist upward at an angle that makes it invisible and therefore impossible to detect or block. Very often when stepping forward into this action, one finds the forearm naturally falls on the opponent's chest in an instinctive effort to fend him off. The Ninja, recognizing this instinctive action, merely built on it to deliver the Palm Heel Strike to the chin of the enemy. Again, no more than four pounds of force need be applied to snap the enemy's head back and cause a whiplash type of injury that will often render him unconscious. The point of the chin is the target, again, the site of a nerve cluster.

Rake Down Across the Eyes

Completing the upward strike to the chin, the Ninja rakes down across the eyes of the opponent with his fingertips. Only a small amount of pressure is required to make the eyes water uncontrollably, effectively blinding the enemy for several minutes. This is the same principle as tear gas. Also, the fingernails inevitably scratch the face, producing a stinging, burning pain, and tearing the skin to produce a type of wound resembling a burn. The application of these steps is collectively known as the Flaming Hand because Qi is mentally projected into the palm, filling it with energy, which often produces a distinct reddish tint to the hand. This is a result of the Fire Hand training method alluded to earlier.

The method requires the student of the Fire Hand, or Iron Sand Palm in some schools, to stand waist deep in water with a 12 x 12 x 1-inch white or yellow pine board floating before him and a cluster of incense sticks hanging over it at the level of the heart. Note how the symbolism is maintained. The heart is the seat of Fire in Chinese medicine. The student holds his palm face down over the boards just below the incense until he feels the heat of the sticks on the back of his hand, whereupon, with fingers loosely curled in the Dragon Fist formation, he "tightens his belly" and slaps down on the center of the board, breaking it cleanly in two. Of course, the board seldom breaks the first time. So a great deal of practice and concentration is required to master this skill.

Rake Down Across the Eyes

It is, however, the exact method used to initiate Kata Dan'te. Namely, the Ninja "kindles the fire" by "tightening his belly" in anticipation of the attack, and this evokes the sensation of heat developed through hours of the Fire Hand training method. He covers his right hand, the one usually trained in this method (some schools require bilateral practice), because he doesn't want the enemy to see his hand turning red and guess how he will respond. He then applies this heat to the head of the enemy, striking with exactly the same sort of action and force he mastered slapping the board in the water and breaking it with four pounds of force. Some schools of martial art teach that one should also exhale the syllable "Haaa!" when making this strike in practice or combat, since among the Six Healing Breaths (*Iron Body Ninja*) "Ha" is the sound of the heart/ Fire. Likewise, this *kiai*, or "spirit-shout," can be used to shock the enemy into faltering. *Kiai* is practiced by "shouting out a candle." In the blinding speed training method, the student is advised to vent all his anger at the enemy and scream the "Ha" sound throughout the ten-second application of fists.

This single technique composed of three separate strikes performed simultaneously is often enough alone to disable any attacker.

Single Fire Palm Strike, Left

Since this is a "book" of techniques, Kata Dan'te continues. It may not be possible to use the Fire Hand just described, because the enemy may have already secured some hold or lock from which the Ninja may have to extricate himself. If so, or if supplementary blows are required, the form provides for a variety of strikes against other sensitive targets. The next, which flows smoothly from the previous position blocking the enemy's arm, is to slide the left Fire Hand down his arm and strike him on the side of the head with an Inverted Palm Strike to the ear.

Likewise, clapping him on the ear would be effective against this target. The palm drives a small column of air into the ear canal, striking the enemy internally, leaving no mark on the skin. Because of the angle of attack, the Inverted Fist is almost impossible to block, even in normal combat. Here, it illustrates the invisible nature of the techniques.

Alternately, the high point of the cheek may be struck with the palm heel, numbing the face by striking the trigeminal nerve, which runs across the bone at that point. The heat

Single Fire Palm Strike, left

generated by the Iron Sand Palm or Fire Hand practice may be transmitted to the enemy's head and face by gripping his cheek with the fingers and squeezing to produce a painful "face-lock" that can be used to subdue an attacker, much like the FBI trick of pinching the upper lip as a "come-along" for wayward detainees. Ancient masters were said to leave a red handprint "burned into the victim's face."

Single Fire Palm Strike, right

Single Fire Palm Strike, Right

Taking advantage of the reciprocal action of drawing the left Inverted Fist back from the eardrum strike, the Ninja twists his hips and shoulders to deliver an Inverted Palm Heel Strike to the left side of the enemy's head. Again, the target may be the trigeminal nerve or the eardrum. This is, in effect, a very awkward slap to the side of the head.

Another application of these two slaps as a single devastating blow, which illustrates the lengths to which the Ninja of old would go to employ Fire as a psychological and physical weapon, was to dip the hands into Plum Wine, a very volatile and flammable liquid of olden times, and pass them through an open flame, setting them on fire. By waving the arms in large circles, the heat of the flame was conducted away from the hands, and the effect was to produce a dazzling hypnotic display to distract the enemy from the incoming technique that followed—namely, slapping both sides of the head at once. The military principle involved is simultaneous flanking attacks. Even if one fails, the odds favor one side breaking through the enemy's defenses and striking a telling blow.

Of course, for our purposes, this is a Double Clap on both ears. With the hands ablaze, however, the ancient Ninja would not only disable the opponent with such a stunning blow, but also set his hair and head on fire. He could then withdraw at leisure or seek other opponents, since his adversary was effectively eliminated and often would attract his mates who would try to save him, taking them out of the battle as well.

Naturally, a single Flaming Hand could serve equally well if one were, say, facing an army on the battlefield. Surely such an amazing feat would cause considerable confusion and might win the day by "magic" instead of a great deal of bloodshed. Further, the Ninja could easily endure the heat on his hand or hands to accomplish this because of the Fire Hand training method given earlier, having accustomed his hands to heat from the incense sticks. The psychological principle in that training is to use the heat from the incense to aid in imagining the "fire rising from the belly" where it was "kindled by tightening the belly" and travels along the channels of the arm to "fire the hand" with Qi. Eventually, the imagination triggers an actual increase in the flow of blood to the hand and slightly anesthetizes it in anticipation of the impact with the board floating on the water.

Dragon Folds Wing, armlock

Dragon Folds Wing, Armlock

Now that the enemy is "engulfed in the flame" of his foolish attack by application of the Fire Hand, he begins to "burn" and collapse into the flame. Scoop under his left arm and catch him by the shoulder as if to help him if he were intoxicated. By so doing, the Ninja could carry the enemy away and sit him quietly down. Or, continue the application of the Fire techniques as in the formal exercise or practice.

Dragon-Mouth Throat Strike

Dragon-Mouth Throat Strike

Now we are going to subdue the fire of the enemy's anger, which led him to this unfortunate circumstance, and once again, notice that this method could be used alone to obtain a "control technique" on the adversary. This will be accomplished by "cutting of the wind" that feeds the fire, a principle often taught in actual fire prevention courses.

Slap the enemy on the sternum, a blow seen in the professional wrestling matches to drive air out of the opponent's chest, and slide the hand upward under the chin, striking the trachea with the web of the hand—the fleshy part between thumb and index finger. This is not a powerful strike as might be described in the blinding speed method, but rather a proven method of obtaining a firm grip on the enemy's throat. Pressure is applied to the carotid artery on either side of the neck by the thumb and the index finger. This cuts off the supply of blood to the brain, rendering the adversary unconscious in a matter of seconds. It will certainly "sap his strength" and discourage further conflict long before he passes out. Note that it is not necessary to close off the windpipe and cause a painful choking hold, which might induce the opponent to struggle violently, to ensure his compliance. The Armlock can be used to numb the arm distally from the armpit or brachial nerve, which runs along the inside of the bicep, by firm fingertip pressure ("putting out a small fire"), and the Heel Lock, which can be augmented to break his balance by pressure against his knee by your knee, holding him in place for what is known in Pa-Kua Chang, "eight trigrams boxing," as the Classic One-Hand Strangle. The opponent will not be harmed if pressure is released when he passes out.

Dragon Stealing a Peach

To "extinguish the fire in his belly" swing the Fire Hand away from his throat and in a large arc, like the swinging arms used in the Flaming Hands Strike, to strike the opponent in the groin with a Palm Up Strike. The heel of the hand impacts against the pubis, a small finger of bone that joins the processes of the pelvis together in front. It lies directly in front of the bladder, which is a stunning blow in itself. The fingers wrap around the testicles and squeeze, using enough pressure to "bring the enemy to his knees" as determined by time and circumstances. As G. Gordon Liddy once said when describing this type of control technique, "When you got 'em by the

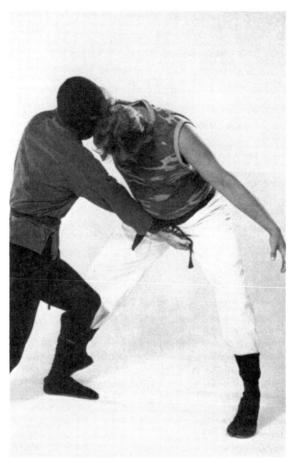

Dragon Stealing a Peach

groonies, their hearts and their minds will follow." This
technique is called Dragon or Monkey Stealing a Peach in those
martial arts that use animal symbolism to classify their techniques instead of elements. In ancient times, Ninja were taught
to execute this strike with the middle finger, symbol of fire,
extended, striking the acupuncture point known as Needle at
the Bottom of the Sea on the base of the torso. This point lies

directly over the prostate gland and, by virtue of the multitude of nerve clusters which meet at this site, sends a shocking, searing pain up the center of the body to stun the heart. Still, no more than four pounds of pressure are needed to render the largest adversary unconscious in this manner. Another metaphor for this technique is "taking the heart" out of the enemy. And again, it is an "internal strike" invisible to the naked eye.

Dragon Wing Strike to Solar Plexus

Dragon Wing Strike to Solar Plexus

As the enemy begins to "crumple into the inferno of his rage" following these aforementioned strikes to his vital and fatal points with four pounds of force or pressure, "stand him back up" by delivering an Elbow Strike to the solar plexus. This point lies on the xyphoid process, a small triangular piece of bone on the tip of the sternum, which may be "knocked back" into the diaphragm by a large surface area blow like the Elbow Strike and impact the phrenic nerve. This nerve runs down the neck behind the ribs to deliver nerve impulses that cause us to breathe. When "jarred" in this manner, those impulses are disrupted, temporarily, causing the diaphragm to cease its bellows action to fill the lungs. This will literally "knock the wind" out of him because he will no longer be breathing. Since the amount of force used is so small, no permanent injury results, usually not even a bruise if the point of the elbow hits the xyphoid properly, and the intercostal muscles between the ribs will still draw in enough air to prevent brain damage, even if he gasps a few times and passes out, unable to "catch his breath."

Dragon Wing Strikes the Jade Pillow

By twisting the hips and stepping slightly back with the right foot, the enemy is pulled into a more secure armlock, and his head is lowered such that a blow may be delivered to the base of the skull with a Downward Elbow Strike. As before, this is such a close-range technique that it is impossible for the opponent to see or defend against it. It is a "fist" that, when applied with four pounds of pressure, either as a blow or steady direct pressure for less than a minute, will render the opponent unconscious. This is often taught in the military as a "sentry-removal technique" and is a favorite target for muggers who use blackjacks or clubs. It jars the skull, banging the brain around in its pan of cerebro-spinal fluid, causing contricule bruising and lacerations to the brain that "cut off the head of the snake" from the rest of the body. Obviously, if the direct pressure method was to be used, it would be necessary to "ride the opponent" down to the mat, pinning his face to the floor by pressing on the back of his neck with the elbow. Another metaphor for this is "rubbing his face in the dirt."

Dragon Wing Strikes the Jade Pillow

Break the Dragon's Wing

When confronted with violence, a Ninja has four options open to him in response. He can stand and take a beating; he can fight back and risk injuring himself or the adversary; he

Break the Dragon's Wing

can run away; or he can "disarm" the aggressor. This applies on all levels, verbal, mental, and physical. There follows in Kata Dan'te a series of techniques intended to demonstrate the disarming aspect of the Fire element known as the "wood chopping" method. It can be applied equally to the leg as well as to the arm, depending on the circumstances of the battle and the amount of force needed to subdue or restrain an aggressor. The principle is to strike at the enemy's joints, especially when they are already hyperextended, as in the armlock. In this case, the elbow of the enemy is trapped between the shoulder of the Ninja and held in place by pressure against the joint. A sharp chopping blow with the edge of the hand, as if chopping with a small ax, is sufficient to cause a severe sprain or strain of the joint. Pressure against the elbow can induce as much pain as needed to ensure cooperation or submission without permanent injury.

Break the Dragon's Shoulder

Break the Dragon's Shoulder

Having hyperextended the elbow, the Ninja delivers a chopping blow to the back of the shoulder. By virtue of the armlock, a moderate blow is enough to dislocate the shoulder anteriorly, effectively ending any further aggression. The shoulder can "pop out of the joint" in a variety of directions. Forward is as painful as any of them, but it can usually be slipped back into place without surgery.

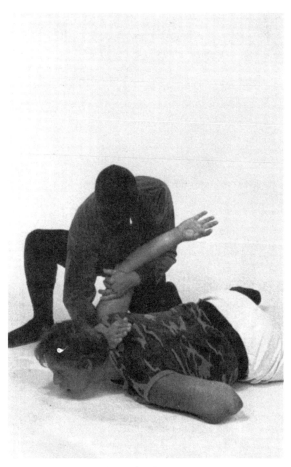

Stun the Dragon

Stun the Dragon

A third chopping blow is executed to the seventh cervical vertebra. This has much the same effect as striking the base of the skull with the elbow. It is a stunning blow that renders the opponent unconscious. Once again, if no more than four pounds of force is used, permanent injury seldom results, even though the vertebrae may be jarred out of place and stun the spinal cord causing temporary paralysis. It takes a lot more force to dislocate the vertebrae and sever the spinal cord if that were the intended effect.

Double Dragon Stamp Kick

Release your armlock and jump on the enemy's back to drive the air out of his lungs or to deliver a double stomp to his back. As with the blow to the seventh cervical vertebra, it takes a lot of force to actually break the spine or rupture any internal organs. The result of "not trying to kill him" but simply stun him into submission would be to bruise any organs landed on, although this is likely to leave an external bruise or swelling over the area of impact. Likewise, a firm stamp with either foot serves the same purpose. In professional wrestling, downed opponents are often "stomped" in this manner, but wrestlers use the "flat of the foot" rather than the heel to lessen injuries in the ring. The blow is invisible because it is delivered from behind the opponent. This would be analogous to sneaking up behind him and executing a Side Kick to the back, if he were standing. The impact is somewhat increased here, since the enemy is "hammered" between the Stamp Kick and the mat.

Double Dragon Fist to Temples

The Double Ear Strike, or Flaming Hands technique, described earlier is simulated in Kata Dan'te by performing it from behind, both hands clapping the ears at the same time. "Setting the hair on fire" is simulated by seizing the hair and

Double Dragon Stamp Kick

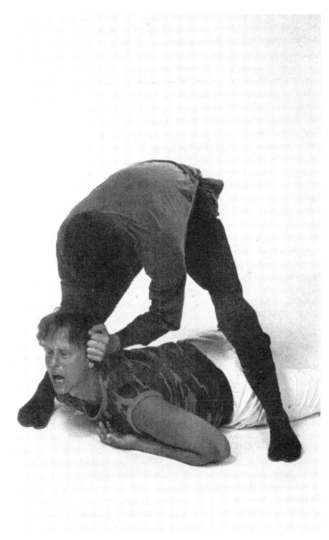

Double Dragon Fist to Temples

pulling sharply back. The scalp is not as sensitive as some other areas of the body, but many an opponent can be led around by pulling his hair. Where the head goes, the body follows.

Ride the Dragon

The second action of simulating the Flaming Hands Strike is performed by slamming the opponent's head onto the mat by means of the Hair Lock. This blow, like the strike to the base of the skull, jars the brain by banging the forehead onto the floor. This is enough to make the opponent "see stars" or sparks if you prefer the Fire symbolism and/or "knock him out" by striking the Third Eye Point above and between the eyebrows with only four pounds of force. This Third Eye Point is also an excellent target for fist or Buffalo Knuckle Strike, if the opponent were standing. Such a blow often causes a large knot to appear on the forehead, the face to turn red, as if afire, and the eyes to close in pain, making the technique one that induces invisibility by temporarily blinding the adversary.

Dragon Wings Across the Sky

Roll the opponent over onto his back by taking a firm hold on his shoulder and hip and stepping back. This is similar to the method used to turn an injured patient onto a backboard by paramedics, taking advantage of leverage to accomplish its purpose. If the opponent were standing, this technique would be a method of "opening him like a door" through which the Ninja could escape, by throwing him aside. Pulling and turning the hips and shoulders at the same time breaks his balance. This is sometimes referred to as "stirring the embers" to see if any "fire" is left in an unconscious opponent or check the condition of a sparring partner stunned by a punch or kick.

Double Dragon Stamp to the Chest

Perform a second Double Stamp Kick to the front of the prone enemy. As before, this would simulate kicks to the body if he were standing. In this case, the effect is to drive the wind

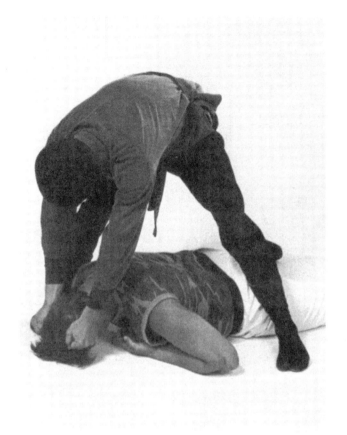

Ride the Dragon

out of his lungs or bruise the internal organs. Stamping on the anterior torso, either with both feet, as shown, or with two Single Stamp Kicks to the upper and lower torso is more likely to cause a serious injury. There are times, however, when a more powerful blow may be required such as when an attacker is drugged or intoxicated with liquor or rage. There are a variety of vital points for the Twelve Organs of Chinese medicine on the torso which may be struck in this manner.

Dragon Wings Across the Sky

Double Dragon Stamp to the Chest

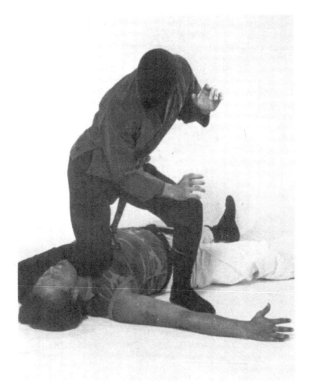

Dragon Drops to Earth

Dragon Drops to Earth

Another method of "choking the enemy into submission" is demonstrated by the next technique. Placing the knee or shin across his throat to apply a strike or pressure against the windpipe is both painful and effective in subduing an attacker. Once again, not a great deal of pressure is required to be effective, but it takes longer for him to pass out from lack of oxygen when he can't breathe than it does when the supply of blood to the brain is cut off as in the One-Hand Strangle. The technique is included because it illustrates the principle of the Choke-Hold Submission method. It is found at this point in the form because it is easy to move into this position from the previous technique, standing on the enemy's chest.

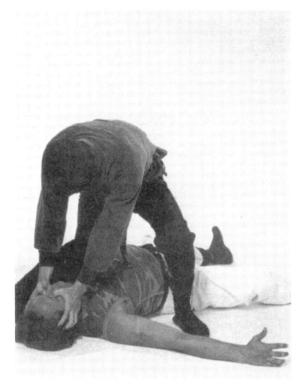

Double Dragon Claw to the Head

Double Dragon Claw to the Head

The Flaming Hands Strike is performed against the enemy's face as he lies prostrate on the mat. One of the reasons for practicing it in this position is that it teaches the Ninja the particular posture, bent over at the waist, arms well forward, that is best suited to applying this technique when the enemy is upright. It will be found, by those who try this technique in combat, that one must indeed duck low and come in under the enemy defenses with the body while the arms swing wide enough to draw his gaze in both directions, creating an effective distraction that allows the twin strike to impact on the targets.

Double Reverse Dragon Claw to the Head

Double Reverse Dragon Claw to the Head

A variation of the Flaming Palms Strike is the Double Reverse Fire Hand Strike. It is intended to be executed "inside the enemy's defenses" as opposed to being a double flanking attack (from both sides at once). Cross the forearms in front of the chest defensively, or in Kata Dan'te, by pulling them back from the last position, and reach forward with the wrists crossed to slap the enemy on both sides of the head at once. With a small amount of practice, the Ninja learns to "widen the gap" between the crossed palms and slap quite soundly on the eardrums as before. The main reason for this variation is to provide an option in case the enemy's defense made the previous method unlikely to succeed. As in the Fire Hand Strike this is an "inner gate" punch.

Dragon Palm Strike

Execute a Palm Heel, or Fire Hand Strike, to the opponent's nose. This is an extremely sensitive point on the anatomy, and even a small amount of force will cause the eyes to water uncontrollably, just as in the Vertical First Strike given elsewhere. Four pounds of pressure is not usually sufficient to break the nose but may cause bleeding, since the blood vessels therein are small and easily damaged by even a moderate blow. A bloody nose is usually enough to end a fight without causing permanent injury.

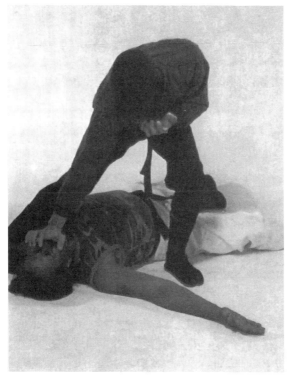

Dragon Palm Strike

The Cross Step

The Cross Step

Stepping over the body of the opponent simulates using the Cross Step to avoid the enemy altogether. Some schools teach that it is the transition step into the Air kata, which begins by taking a diagonal step forward in much the same manner in order to "circle" the opponent or "turn his corner" evasively. In the Fire element form given here, it signals the end of the dance.

It should be noted by the clever student, that much of this kata involves having the adversary, or patient, lying on his back or stomach. This is to facilitate study of the vital and fatal points, just as if the opponent were a patient instead of an attacker. Different ryu (schools) teach different targets on the torso, front or back, which may be attacked with four pounds of force or direct pressure against the acupuncture point designated, depending on the preference of the sensei. Such points as the tip of the lowest rib on the right, for example, is the "alarm point" for the liver, which lies directly below it. A blow to this area can stun an opponent and knock him out. In boxing circles it is known as a left hook to the liver. By the same token the tip of the lowest rib on the left is the alarm point, meaning it becomes spontaneously tender when the underlying organ is diseased or swollen, for the spleen. A blow to this area can rupture the underlying organ and cause internal bleeding, without leaving a mark on the surface of the skin—another example of the Invisible Fist. Alarm points may also be used to tonify or sedate the underlying organ in Chinese medicine and acupuncture. There are twelve such alarm points, one for each of the Twelve Organs.

It is this knowledge of the anatomy and his understanding of psychology, both his own and that of an aggressor, that enables the Ninja to turn himself into a virtual or symbolic Fire Breathing Dragon, capable of "meeting fire with fire" through force of will and development of self-confidence through practice and study; capable of venting the blazing inferno of his rage against an attacker and quite literally "burning him down to the ground"; or gently subduing him by pressure against the nerve plexes that represent Fire in Chinese medicine. All this because he does not limit his practice to one method of performing kata, but rather varies it—the better to explore all the ramifications and subtleties hidden within. It is simply a question of how much force he believes is required at the time.

THE BREATH WEAPON

In his book *Secret Fighting Arts of the World,* author John Gilbey tells the story of a master of the martial arts who had the secret of knocking out his opponent with an attack by *halitosis*! This man, he claimed, had long ago decided that he was not one for physical confrontation and so devised a method of creating and retaining in his bowels a particularly putrid odor, guaranteed to bowl over the strongest man by overloading the olfactory lobes of the brain. These are located directly above the nose, and are virtually unprotected from this type of attack, hence the pronounced effect of tear gas, mustard gas, adamcite, and other airborne agents. The olfactory lobes actually extend out from the underside of the brain and are almost like antennae when seen in dissection.

Gilbey, not detecting any offensiveness on the part of this individual, asked him to demonstrate, whereupon the master belched in the face of the author, who promptly passed out.

In many ways, this is similar to the Blow in the Face, except that technique relies on tactile stimulation of the eyelids, whereas this one acts directly on the nervous system.

For those individuals whose education was so limited in childhood that they did not learn to belch on command, we include the following technique known in Chinese medicine as Swallowing Air, and is used to expel noxious gases from the stomach that may result from contaminated food or poor digestion.

Since the stomach is inflatable, being a Yin, or "hollow," organ, take a deep breath and swallow, or inhale while swallowing, to fill it with air. The hiatal sphincter, at the level of the solar plexus, is the constricting muscle that prevents the contents of the stomach from regurgitating during digestion. It is also the stricture that traps gases in the stomach that are produced by the chemical reaction of foodstuffs and digestive acids. Heartburn is a condition resulting from an overproduction of such gases and pressure on the hiatal area. As sufferers will attest, a good belch often relieves this pressure, and the pain subsides. To practice burping, gulp down a carbonated soft drink and regulate the amount of gas expelled by gently tensing the belly.

Dragon Breath is a technique not unknown in the wrestling arena. Furthermore, in gladiatorial times, some contestants would purposely not bathe for days prior to a match, making it unsavory to grapple with them. Relying on this psychological advantage, some lived to win freedom, if not popularity. In the same way, using distasteful oils and foul-smelling necklaces of garlic inhibit an enemy's aggressiveness because he is uncomfortable with this type of defense or attack.

It is worthwhile to practice the belching technique even if one has no wish to develop the chemical formula that goes with it, since it will be needed in the final stage, the Book of Wood.

SILENT *KIAI*

In Karate, at the conclusion of the *kiai*, the abdomen is taut and most of the air is forced out of the lungs by dynamic tension. In the same way, learning how to expel a ball of air from the abdomen makes it possible to snuff out a candle from a much greater distance than by blowing at it. This is accomplished by holding the mouth open in the same manner used to "shout out" the candle rather than by pursing the lips, as in the first method.

Stand facing the candle at arm's length in a Horse Stance with your mouth open. Inhale deeply. Project the Qi at the flame by sharply contracting the abdomen. This will send out larger amounts of air than would puffing through the lips with the diaphragm. In martial arts, this is called Silent *Kiai*, or Dragon Breath, and is considered a "gas" attack, thus, its classification with the Fire element.

4

THE BOOK OF AIR

"The Sword of the Mind"

The "power to cloud men's minds" is the goal of the Dragon-Style Invisible Fist: to "put the idea of Fire in the mind of the enemy," to make him hesitate and reconsider his acts without resorting to physical force to restrain him and make him more reasonable.

To accomplish this, the Ninja looked to the next element, Air. The Sky Dragon techniques include the jumping and flying kicks seen in other martial arts styles, as well as circular fist techniques based on the wing-flap action of a flying dragon, and the Poison Gas Breath, described later in this section. The primary symbolism employed, however, is that of Air representing the mind. For that reason, the techniques of Hsi-Men-Jitsu ("sigh-men-jet-su"), the Way of the Mind Gate, are classified and taught at this level. They include psychology, hypnotism, and illusion.

Bear in mind that the Chinese dragon is much different from the European version. The latter was always guarding virgins or gold—two items for which he had no use whatsoever—usually at the behest of an evil wizard, while in Chinese astronomy, the constellation known as Red Dragon, a sign of coming rains and rebirth, appears in the night sky every spring. In Ninjitsu, "riding the wind" refers to the various exercises used to develop telepathic abilities.

THE TRANCE

The best opportunity for using this technique is during a group discussion of Ninjitsu or psychic powers, when the mood is already established. Select a volunteer from the group. Sit quietly for a moment to create a relaxed state. Then simply tell the subject that when the magician says the magic word, or cue, the subject will be in a relaxed, trancelike state for a few seconds and will not see the performer move out of his line of vision. When the subject blinks and comes out of this posthypnotic suggestion, the Ninja seems to have vanished before his very eyes!

Of course, onlookers are treated to the show and are amazed at the effectiveness of the technique. Notice that no magic power is alluded to in the hypnotic state, only a simple instruction, usually less than nine words and seldom more than three.

The subject, like many who participate in stage hypnotism acts, may later claim that he was just going along, but the technique is nonetheless a great crowd-pleaser. After all, why should the subject go out of his way to make the magician look good? Perhaps because he, too, believes on some level that the individual has some secret power, and that if he plays along he may gain some insight into this greater mystery. Then it becomes a matter of enlightened self-interest.

This is like another "mental" trick, in which an unprepared spectator is asked onstage and told to choose a card from a display. A prediction of which card will be chosen has been previously recorded. When the spectator goes behind the display table he sees that one card is lying on top of a dollar bill. Guess which one he will pick!

Could it be that he is actually powerless for the moment to prevent the "command" sent to him by the mentalist? If that is the case, then any later claim of denial is actually a defense mechanism designed to save face and self-esteem. To be sure, it is as plausible an explanation as any.

For the Ninja, it matters not one bit! Regardless which explanation is true, as long as it is an effective technique, it should be studied, evaluated, and experimented with. Just the ability to transmit the command *Blink!* would be enough to let one escape, and among the Wind techniques of the Ninja, such tricks as the mind-whip and blank-wall meditation, based on the same principle of suggestibility, are included.

HYPNOSIS

Like all physical techniques, mental ones require a certain amount of practice and preparation. Hypnotism is only one tool.

Inducing a trance (A)

Inducing a Trance (A)

The subject and the Ninja sit facing each other in the Seiza, the meditation kneeling position. The Ninja fixes the gaze of the subject and has him take a few deep breaths to develop a feeling of rapport and relaxation. The Ninja speaks in a soft, hypnotic tone, speaking only to the subject and ignoring any outside distractions. This cues the subject to do likewise.

The Ninja places suggestions of relaxation and sleep in the mind of the subject. He does this using alliteration, emphasizing certain sounds and syllables. In this case, the same one is used as that to dispel fear, the "shhh" or wind-breath sound. He likewise harmonizes his breath to that of the subject, then slowly changes the pattern to one of slow, deep, relaxing respiration.

Inducing a trance (B)

Inducing a Trance (B)

With a simple hypnotic gesture, the Ninja has the subject close his eyes. Note that the downward action and the proximity of the fingertips to the subject's face, as well as the rapport and avoidance of outside distractions, not only induce, but virtually compel him to comply with this simple command.

The subject is now, technically, in a hypnotic trance. He has psychologically demonstrated his trust in the Ninja not to injure or embarrass him as long as he participates in the experiment. Having closed his eyes, he is now dependent on the Ninja for direction. He closed his ears when he began ignoring distractions. Now he must "feel" his way, and depends on the Ninja to guide him.

Inducing a trance (C)

Inducing a Trance (C)

The Ninja then performs a simple test to insure that the subject is hypnotized and to demonstrate to the onlookers that the subject is under his "spell." Psychologically, this is when the subject proves his "loyalty" by following orders without question. The Ninja could be directing him to put his hand in a fire. He cannot see, so he does not know what he is doing. Nevertheless, he trusts the Ninja, achieved through the suggestibility stage, and so will now obey commands. This is a powerful position of trust and should *never* be abused. To do so is to invite misfortune.

The arm levitation test determines the degree of compliance of the subject. Specifically, he will be raising and lowering his arm on cue, but the Ninja first makes him aware of the coming command and builds to it slowly with his suggestions of the subject's arm (right or left) feeling light. This can be easily suggested if the relaxation exercise also suggests that the body feels light. Then the Ninja gradually suggests that it is light enough to float: "In fact, you can almost feel it floating now. It is so light that it *is* floating. Don't resist it, let your arm lift upward, slowly, carefully, easily." He continues until the command is obeyed. When everyone is satisfied that the subject is hypnotized, give the subject praise for relaxing and letting his arm float, which rewards the effort, and then suggest that his arm is returning to normal, and let it settle back onto his thigh.

After placing the posthypnotic suggestion in the mind of the subject, the Ninja directs him to forget all memory of the hypnotic state until a specific cue is given. He then awakens the subject by counting from one to three or by clapping his hands.

Upon ending the trance, the Ninja questions the subject to insure that he will obey the posthypnotic command by (a) pretending that the entire experiment has not yet happened and eliciting a verbal response from the subject that he has done nothing as yet. Again, this "proves" that the subject, by agreeing with the Ninja/hypnotist, will continue to "play his part" in the show. Or, (b) by thanking the subject for his participation and eliciting a verbal response that he feels better and more relaxed than before. Either summation may be employed; the key is for the subject to agree with what the hypnotist says, even after the "trance" is ended.

The Ninja congratulates the subject on his success and performance, and tells him that the experiment is concluded. They may now stand up.

THE CUE

After being seated for even five minutes, you may find that standing causes a sudden feeling of light-headedness, as the heart must accelerate to pump blood higher to the head, and the blood that was "squeezed" out of the legs by kneeling must be replaced, so one should stand up slowly. This, however, is an excellent opportunity to cue the subject, because his vision will already be somewhat dimmed and the blood rushing to his head will disorient him. Also, the quicker the cue is used, the more likely it is to be effective. The longer you wait, the greater the chance he will forget it or stop looking for it. Furthermore, the rapport that was established during the trance is still in effect, though it, too, fades with time.

Stepping out of sight (A)

Stepping Out of Sight (A)

The Ninja gives his subject the same visual cue used to have the subject close his eyes, that of wiping the hand downward in front of the subject's face. Unlike using this gesture to make him blink so you can duck away as in some of the previous techniques, the gesture to "close the eyes" may be used at a greater distance, since the intention is to confirm his compliance to the verbal contract rather than physically *make* him blink by proximity of the hand to his face. Next he gives the verbal cue, which is stronger and for which the subject was prepared through the hypnotic gesture, and returns him to the trance.

The verbal cue may be a simple word suggestion, like "Sleep," or may be a "magical"/nonsense word, like "Afghanistan Banana Stand," or gibberish that would not ever be heard in "real" life. Such a magic word would be suggested to the subject during the trance state.

Stepping out of sight (B)

Stepping Out of Sight (B)

The hypnotic trancelike state is indicated by the fixed gaze of the subject. Remember, the blood is rushing from his head, his vision is blurred, and he may be slightly off balance. He is given the preparatory command, then the command for a test he knew was coming but didn't expect so soon. His eyes are still open, so they "roll" out of focus and he stares ahead, unmoving, which gives him a chance to regain his senses. He may or may not "see" the movement of the Ninja as he steps out of sight behind him, but he does not move or react, because that would violate the verbal contract entered into when he volunteered.

Stepping out of sight (C)

Stepping Out of Sight (C)

The subject, acting on the posthypnotic suggestion, returns to full wakefulness in accordance with the secret instructions given to him by the Ninja, and looks around in search of the Ninja, who appears to have suddenly vanished.

The subject will not see the Ninja again until he wishes to reappear, gives the next cue, or steps into view dramatically, thus concluding the presentation. Finish with a bow to the subject, which he may or may not return, your way of thanking him for his cooperation. Also bow to the audience.

Thus, you have taken another step in learning the "power to cloud men's minds." The fifth level, Wood, will enable you, without the hypnotic ritual, to project the "mist," or "fog," into the mind of any foe so that you will be invisible to the eyes of men and genii. There is, however, still a bit more to learn about Air.

THE VOLUNTEERS

Magicians and mesmerists are quite fond of making magical passes over the body and directing its energy with their hands.

Some of this is showmanship, and misdirection. Hypnotists use visual cues and directions, while faith healers maintain that a subtle magnetic field surrounds the body, and that this field may be manipulated by the electrically charged palms or fingers of the physician. More on this field later.

In the case of actual stage hypnotism, the master of the mystic arts selects a group of volunteers from the audience. Most of these people are extroverts who enjoy participating in events for which they can receive applause. Shy people don't volunteer and are seldom even coaxed onstage. Nor should they be, because their own self-consciousness will contribute to clumsiness and a half-hearted effort.

It should be recalled that the stage is the "home court" of the magician, while the average theater-goer is relatively uncomfortable there. This, together with the preconceived notion that the performer is in some way possessed of mysterious powers, combines to create the impression that the magician has control of the situation in the minds of viewers and participants. This is true. He is in command, partly because he chooses to be, partly because he chooses the volunteers, and it doesn't take but once to spot a smart-aleck looking to upstage you.

Upon this pool of volunteers he performs a series of simple tests to determine if they will follow his directions, and which obey best. If they compete with him, they are "allowed" to go back to their seats and enjoy the rest of the show. From the remaining group, he selects a few who will play the part of clowns and actors at his stage direction. He then puts them through a set of simple commands designed to entertain the audience and let the players have a bit of fun.

Almost always, the hypnotist states at the outset, "I will not injure or embarrass you in any way, as long as you assist me in the demonstration of the hypnotic art." This is a verbal contract to which both agree. The hypnotist then gives the person his permission to act silly, dance, sing, react to imaginary heat or cold, withstand tests of strength, pain, and leverage, or impersonate famous personalities (he must be able to deduce which of the volunteers are able to do this and which celebrities they can imitate). This permission is conveyed to the audience by the hypnotic pass: waving the hand before the eyes, verbal suggestions of tiredness and sleep, speaking in a low monotonous voice, or counting backwards. All may be used, and all contribute to the rapport between the hypnotist and subject(s).

The audience is vicariously relaxed as well, since each person theoretically empathizes with one or more of the players. This puts them in a receptive mood to believe what is said onstage. It is what is known as suspension of disbelief: the audience agrees not to look too closely for flaws and allows itself to be amused by the antics of those who have surrendered their will to the stage director or hypnotist.

Actually, when questioned later, almost every one of the volunteers will claim that he or she did feel a bit relaxed but never really felt under a spell of any sort. They were just "going along with the gag," but some of the others *were* really under. Whether this is true or not is always debatable, since the effect is the same either way. It really makes no difference, because the goal was to put on a good show, and if everyone believed he was "under," then so much the better.

The only real danger lies in using volunteers who try to steal the show by upstaging the hypnotist. This can lead to a verbal, even physical, confrontation, but the usual result is that the smart-aleck makes faces and mocks the hypnotist behind his back. At the very least it is disruptive, although it can be entertaining.

The magician or hypnotist usually awakens his volunteers with a snap of the fingers. If their eyes are closed, this is an auditory signal to open them. Of course, he tells them so verbally and may even count upward from one to three so that they are not startled by the sound. If their eyes are open, this is the signal for them to blink, giving the impression of waking up from a nap or light sleep. All this adds to the illusion of having control of a subject's mind, when in reality it is a series of simple stage directions and psychological leverage.

FINGER-SNAPPING DEFENSE

To the Ninja, the self-defense application of this technique lies in snapping the fingers in the face of an opponent or attacker to make him blink. The eyes have the most sensitive nerve endings in the body; much of the nervous system is devoted to responses that protect the head and eyes. Blinking when a sharp sound is made near the face is only one of them.

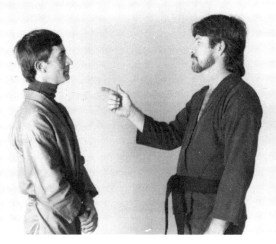

Finger snapping (A)

Finger Snapping (A)

The aggressor makes a threatening or dominating gesture. From this range, he could easily use a single- or needle-finger poke to the eye, which is as good a technique as any given here. Boxers sometimes use the thumb of their glove to blur an opponent's vision in the ring.

Finger Snapping (B)

Deflect the attacker's hand. Do not slap it away, as this would be an escalation of the confrontation. Simply swing your hand upward at moderate speed, with your fingers in a preparatory position to snap until they come into his line of vision, about nose level. This is called a shoulder block.

Finger snapping (B)

Finger Snapping (C)

Snap the fingers as close to his nose as possible. As with the vertical punch, the idea is to get as close as possible without appearing to be a threat. Note that until this moment you were still out of effective striking range.

Finger Snapping (D)

Immediately turn your hand palm down and stab your index and middle fingers into his eyes to blind him with the Two Dragons Seek the Pearl Technique, also known as the Finger Jab. Do not stiffen your fingers. It is unnecessary and may cause injury to the user as well as the aggressor.

A miss will make him blink if he did not do so when you snapped your fingers. A light blow will cause eye watering and temporary pain. A poke will do the same, plus cause shock trauma to the eye. A stab accomplishes all of the above as well as lacerations from the fingernails. A thrust causes dislodge-

ment or collapse of the eyeball. Withdraw your hand immediately. For the technique to be effective, one must practice
ducking out of sight as soon as this reflex is elicited. Better to
look back and see how badly he is hurt when safely out of
range—depending on the level of threat, of course.

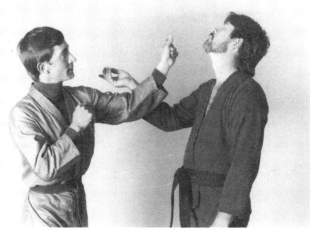

Finger snapping (C)

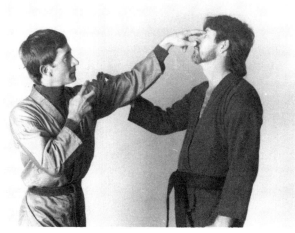

Finger snapping (D)

THE EYE FLICK

A technique based on the same involuntary blink response is
the eye flick. This was first introduced to the American public
on the TV show *Longstreet*, starring James Franciscus as the title
character.

During several episodes, the famous martial artist, Bruce
Lee, was a guest star. He was introduced as a Kung Fu expert to
whom Longstreet turned to learn self-defense after he was
beaten up by a dock worker. Mr. Longstreet, a New Orleans
attorney, had been blinded by a bomb but continued to right
wrongs and punish evil doers.

Lee showed him a variety of techniques, throws, takedowns,
and knee and elbow strikes, all honed and practiced as much as
possible in one sixty-minute drama—and all tailored for use by
a blind man. The one technique Longstreet would not use was
the Eye Flick. He would not endanger the opponent's sight,
since he had lost his own.

He did eventually settle the score with his adversary, returning to the harbor to look him up for a rematch. After a few false
starts, he was "forced" to use the Eye Flick to save himself and
win—*but* he did win! The lesson is that at the time and place
where you make such a stand, if you ever have to, you must
determine how much force is required and be desperate
enough to use it to survive, and realize that whatever you did
must have been the "right" thing to do, because it's what you
did at that time.

Eye Flick (A)

Stand with your shoulder toward your opponent in the
Hidden Hand Stance, given in the second chapter so you
present a smaller target, left palm covering right fist, as though
the right will be the weapon. (This is a follow-up to or
alternative method of delivering the Buffalo Knuckle or Phoenix Eye Fist.)

Eye flick (A)

Eye Flick (B)

When the enemy punches, deflect his arm by shifting forward and letting it strike your lead shoulder. This puts you in range for striking with your lead hand. Swing your left hand out and around as when using the hand flash. Note that in that example the enemy threw a left punch, while in this one he throws a right. Observe that this is virtually the same technique against both punches, the only difference being that this strike is "inside" his defense instead of "outside," blocking his attack downward. The wrist is bent as in the *kasumi* method, with the fingers hidden (curled back out of sight), forming the Chicken Neck Fist, which uses the back of the wrist for striking.

Eye Flick (C)

Suddenly stop the arc of his left arm and flick the backs of the fingertips to strike his eye from the side. This is much less likely to cause injury, but guarantees that he will blink. This may be used as a probing attack jab, or a vanishing technique, or followed up with the stunning Phoenix Eye Fist.

Note also that both of these are circular in nature, in keeping with with the elemental principles. As is customary, the prac-

Eye flick (B)

Eye flick (C)

tice method is Snuffing Out a Candle with the hand-whip or Eye Flick.

The Eye Flick is difficult to block or deflect because of the sudden acceleration of the fingers. Like cracking a whip, all the motion of the arm is transferred to its end, providing a sharp snapping motion. Since this is initiated at a range of about three inches, it is much too fast to see, hence the saying, "the hand is quicker than the eye"—one-fiftieth of a second to blink.

Let the recoil bring the hand back even faster than it was whipped out, safely out of range and prepared to lash out again if need be, or launch the real attack. This motion is exactly like the Karate Backfist, in which the strike is delivered with the backs of the first two knuckles. The popping, snapping motion of this punch is so deceptive that it is forbidden in the professional boxing ring. Muhammad Ali used it extensively as a sort of swatting, brushing jab, not only confusing opponents by making himself hard to see but also infuriating them by constantly rubbing his glove in their face. Even though these punches did not score points or have a telling effect, they were, nonetheless, excellent examples of using the Invisible Fist.

FLICKING OUT THE CANDLE

The practice method is flicking out the candle. By this time, having developed this skill with several other fists, you will find this one simple. The force of the wind generated by this fist is much larger and stronger than a closed fist. See how easy invisibility can be?

Flicking Out Candle (A)

Stand with your shoulder aimed at the candle in the Mi Chuan, or Hidden Hand Stance. Relax your wrist and let your hand drop limply away from covering your right fist. Tighten the belly.

Flicking Out Candle (B)

Strike out on the exhalation, aiming the back of your wrist at the target. With your fist closed, your hand is four to six inches shorter than with the fingers extended. With the fingers extended and the wrist curled back, the hand is eight to ten inches shorter than with full reach of the fingertips. Your eye will see the back of your wrist and act in response to its distance from your eye in terms of spatial distance and speed.

Flicking out candle (A)

Flicking out candle (B)

Flicking out candle (C)

Flicking Out Candle (C)

Whip your fingers toward the flame, snuffing it out with a quick snapping action. When your arm is extended but your elbow not locked straight out, flick out the backs of your fingertips to strike your opponent on the temple or ear. By overshooting in this manner you virtually assure that you will at least strike the side of his nose, even if he is skilled in slipping punches. Most people, even boxers, will react to a hand coming at their face with a ducking or blocking movement as soon as the attack is perceived. Therein lies the key.

Snap your hand back as quickly as it was whipped out to extinguish the candle.

BREATH BLOWGUNS

One final word should be said regarding the use of the breath to propel missiles other than the green mist alluded to earlier. Notably, very short blowguns are used by some Ninja Ryu to shoot tiny darts at the eyes of an opponent. The Ninja also practice the technique of Spitting Needles by curling the tongue into a shallow trough, or V shape, and placing the dart in the tunnel for launching.

An easier method is Spewing Caltrops From the Mouth, but again, these sharp little three-corner nails must be carried in the mouth most of the time and always present the danger of being swallowed accidentally.

These are only a few of the methods used by the Ninja of feudal Japan to protect their identities. If they were captured, any attempt to remove their masks would result in the expulsion of any one of several projectiles into the eyes of the enemy, not only making identification difficult but also providing an opportunity to escape by vanishing.

THE SHOUT

When faced with an imminent confrontation, it is often advisable to "steal the march" from the adversary and attempt to overcome him verbally before he can become belligerent enough to make an attack.

Haraki: the spirit shout

Haraki: the Spirit Shout

As the enemy is preparing to attack, so is the Ninja. He draws air into the Tan T'ien and tenses the belly. Using the command voice, he shouts a single-word order to halt or move, bringing the shout up from the center and directing the forceful blast of air directly at the face and eyes of the aggressor, who should flinch.

When using the most basic method, the *kiai*, most schools hold that "Ha!" is the best word to yell. It is the sound of the heart.

When using *haraki*, the word is not even heard; it is the sound waves that produce the effect. As seen in the Book of Fire, true Dragon Breath requires expelling foul odors by belching.

The effect, however, of making the enemy fall back without physical contact is identical in these three methods. Punching or Shouting Out the Candle is the test of this ability.

5

THE BOOK OF WOOD

"The Power to Cloud Men's Minds"

Thus far, we have described four of the five primeval elements, Earth, Water, Fire, and Air. They are taught in that order because this is the sequence in which they appear naturally on the fingers of the hand. In Kuji Kiri, the finger-knitting exercises of Ninja meditation, the initial exercise is to place the fingertips together to connect the psychic channels and acupuncture meridians for health and longevity. The pinky, or little finger, represents Earth; the ring, or third, finger symbolizes Water; the middle finger is Fire; and the index finger is Air; and they are joined in that order. The thumb symbolizes and connects the channels and meridians that relate to the Wood element and is touched last. The palms are then pressed together to connect the Dragon and Tiger cavities to form the Praying Hands Mudra, found in every religion throughout time, and even today.

Of the Five Elements, two, Earth and Fire, are considered by Chinese scholars to be "linear" in the direction and nature of their operation. Earth is solid, like a mountain, and cannot be moved or uprooted, while fire is an advancing, consuming force, driven forward by Wind, appetite or fuel, i.e., Wood. This is a fundamental concept in the Law of the Five Elements, the basis for both military strategy and Chinese holistic medicine.

In accordance with the Chinese pattern of categorizing things in corresponding pairs of opposites, it then follows that the other two, Water and Air, are circular in nature, and this can be clearly seen by watching water flow in and around obstacles, and air blowing through open spaces. Both follow the path of least resistance, whereas Earth and Fire offer the most resistance, one by refusing to change or be budged, the other by moving and changing everything in its path.

Balance, then, between and among these forces, is represented by a spiral—circular motion about a linear axis. To primitive man, who first codified these principles, the best way to symbolize this type of motion was to refer to Wood, since the tree grows upward and its leaves and branches and downward (linearly) with its roots. The point of intersection between these two vortices is the ground, just as it is with any whirlpool or tornado, which are also spirals. The tree grows in a progressive ring pattern, showing the circular action of Wood. Together, linear and circular motion represent spiral motion—a pattern of the Universe that is only now being found to exist even by modern science in the electromagnetic forces of life itself. (The ancients, however, knew it all along.)

Kata Dan'te (Fire Breathing Dragon Technique) is not an end in itself. Fire Breathing is but one way of achieving practical immortality, that is to say, good health and longevity.

Those who seek to follow the Silent Way recognize that it is only one way and that becoming an inferno of rage is only one part—the Fire aspect. One must have Water, the empathy to understand why this person has become so unbalanced that he must resort, usually in frustration, to physical violence. Also essential is the Mind Sword, the Air element, to bridge the gap to him and prevent him from injuring himself or others. Nor is

Earth to be neglected; this is the physical bridge between the psychological and the tactile.

Wood, then, represents the penultimate techniques of the Invisible Fist system, the highest expression of the principles upon which any subject, medicine, philosophy, or combat so classified can be presented, because it is a combination of all the "lesser" elements that interact to form the (spiral) pattern of the Universe.

Thus it can be seen that in the symbolic lexicon of the ancient Ninja masters, Wood represented the ultimate expression of harmony with nature and was used to designate the highest level of technique. The expression of this is found in both the martial arts applications and also in the philosophical teachings which form the foundation of Chinese medicine and meditation; the "other side" of the Ninja coin. For, not only are the shadow-warriors the most fearsome fighters, but also the most efficient healers.

To develop all these qualities in coordination the seeker must make the Inner Journey. Only in this way can one come to "know thyself." Only then can one know the rage that all humans are capable of and the compensatory compassion to balance it. Only then will one realize that the "enemy" is only a reflection of the Self, as yet unaware of its motivation or place in the Universe.

The one who has made this journey then has the duty to share this knowledge with ten others. Not all need it, nor all want it. Sometimes, however, you meet another seeker when he makes a challenge and you recognize yourself at his stage. Be gentle. Hurting him is only a way of hurting yourself. In fact, some people lose because they would rather hurt themselves or let someone else hurt them than harm anyone else. This is self-destructive, the opposite of being overly aggressive.

We have seen how man ingests various types of energy—Air, Water, Earth, even Fire—in the form of nutrients. There is a higher level still to be explored and considered—the spiritual.

MANY PATHS

Every major religion teaches the same message. Every style of Karate has as its ultimate goal enlightenment, i.e., understanding why we do what we do and why the world is like it is. Even the wandering hermits of ancient China, who may have seemed lost and alone, were following some inner path in the direction of self-actualization. To them we attribute the longevity exercises.

There is an instinctual need and a motivational drive inherent in humans to understand their world. In learning this, man strives for perfection, always just beyond reach, and so recognizes the limitless potential of mankind. Abraham Lincoln once said, "God could not have created so perfect a work as Man to exist only for an instant. No, Man was meant for immortality." This is so.

Along this path are other seekers, each following his or her own course. Some are at higher levels and act as guides. Those who understand are teachers, and those who do not understand are obstacles, who provide the tests and trials along the way. You were once one of them, but now you *know*.

For this reason, the Ninja learns to control himself so that others will be controlled by following his example. Nevertheless, even to attempt such a course is not for the many.

The wisest of the ancient Chinese philosophers recognized that most people are too concerned with survival to pursue the Silent Way of contemplation and meditation. So it fell to the few to preserve that art, practice it, and share it with those who wish to learn.

THE PATH OF PEACE

The reason the Ninja are so savage and terrifying in war and why they are masters of invisible action is so that war does not occur. Understanding oneself makes it possible to understand others. When this happens, one is said to have compassion and mercy, and one can see that the only good thing about a war is that it has an end. There are those who think violence is not only an answer but, indeed, *the* answer. The truth is, though, that by attacking others they bring about their own downfall.

It is said that "he who lives by the sword dies by the sword." Do not the concepts of karma and the Eightfold Path teach that whatsoever we send into the lives of others comes back into our own three times? All religious sects have some interpretations of the phrase "Do unto others as you would have them do unto you." Is it not obvious that this is the key to peace, harmony, and universal brotherhood?

If we are harsh with ourselves, we are also very hard on others, expecting them to conform to our ideas of perfection, which even we cannot achieve. On the other hand, if we are gentle and have confidence in ourselves, can we not trust others and discover that the wonder of the Universe is its diversity and the ways in which those differences combine to create meaning and beauty? So we have become the Hidden Dragon, concealed in the Earth; kindled by the inner fire in the Golden Stove by breathing (Air); mixed with the Qi and the Juice of Jade (Water); ready and capable of springing to our aid from its concealed forest glade of serenity at an instant's notice. Who else can claim such an ally?

HARNESSING THE WILL

These techniques of behavior modification, in this instance used for the development of self-confidence, are not limited to the martial arts. Indeed, they are found in all self-help books on every topic from losing weight to stopping smoking. All that is required is to tie the desired outcome to the appropriate cue and wait for an opportunity to try it out. It is as automatic as the eye blink response, whereby invisibility on the physical level is attained.

Ninja are taught that if the enemy is angry (Fire), one can fan the flames of his anger and cause him to overcommit to his attack or even become so enraged that he is unable to attack, by using taunts that play on his fears. This is considered an application of Wind (intellect) to Fire (anger). Conversely, one can extinguish the flames by using Water (emotion) by appealing to the enemy's self-interest, or through expressions of sympathy and support with the counsel of patience. This gives the aggressor a way out with dignity—the path of least resistance. This system is known as the Five Feelings and the Five Desires and, like almost everything else, is based on the Five Elements.

The information and techniques given here are no mystery. They are just usually so covered with promises of success that they become diluted and lost. This is the way to become the master of your fate, to have power and responsibility for your own life instead of being a puppet dancing on the strings of the few. That is why it has been kept hidden—until now.

No matter what the goal, if one sets out for it and perseveres in a single-minded manner, it can be achieved. Anything is possible if you have enough will and enough time.

You have learned many new things and acquired many new skills. After those accomplishments, few other challenges can stand in your way. For you know now that the Dragon is within you, that when the need arises you are the Dragon. You have also learned to harness the will, to be patient, and to endure, and these are not powers to be taken lightly. Prisoners of war have told of how they saved their sanity by building a "dream house" in their minds.

Part of this process is the study and exploration of unfamiliar or seemingly strange realms or arts, such as Ninjitsu, so that no possibility, however remote, is overlooked in the quest for understanding. Also part of this process is "creating a ritual," a set of cues, a pattern that will lead to the desired result, like the Cha-no-Yu (Tea Ceremony) or the practice kata of a swordsman. It should be simple and elegant so that it can be easily performed, allowing the mind to dwell on the history, etiquette, and symbolism of the artifacts.

The largest part of the process, however, is in its practice. The old ones knew many ways of teaching and of thinking, but they were also aware of spontaneous insight, gained by hours of rote repetition. It is this sudden realization that is called *enlightenment*.

The "internal work" of ancient Chinese alchemists is often mistaken for magic. Indeed, the scrolls that described the process of turning lead into gold were completely misread by the medieval scientists who "discovered" distillation from the Chinese. They were, in fact, texts on the collection, cultivation, and circulation of the vital life force. Lead, gold, and mercury were symbols of inner energy, not real metals. Distillation to refine the Qi and extract its essence can be used on many levels (which is why so many alchemists of old were alcoholics).

MAGIC SPELLS

Spell casting, or ritual magic, is an important aspect of Hsi-Men-Jitsu, the Way of the Mind Gate. One must take care not to program negative thoughts or emotions, as these are harmful, not to the supposed victim of the spell but rather to the spell caster himself. "Whatever you send into the lives of others comes back to your own three times." is an old Ninja saying. Furthermore, "You always get what you wish for, it is just a matter of time." The person you wish injury upon today may be a friend next week. Then, if he should be hurt, you will feel guilty. This is true even if one puts great store in the theory of coincidence, which would maintain that you wished for something to happen because it was meant to happen anyway. It always comes back to haunt you. Therefore, most spells are for self-improvement.

Many magic rituals begin with a banishing ritual, or the scribing of the mystic pentagram (Five Elements symbol) on the

THE BOOK OF WOOD

floor to "protect" one from demons. It is not any external force that threatens the user of magic; it is the creatures of the id—his own selfishness, greed, envy, cruelty, and so on. These are the Dragons that must be harnessed if one is to know oneself.

Most spells have three or more components, a magic word (mantra, incantation, or verbal); a talisman (symbol, artifact, or visual); and a gesture (kinesthetic, mudra, or posture). Some also require representations of the Five Elements: cups for Water, wand for Fire, sword for Air, coins for Earth, and the lemniscate, or sign of infinity, a figure-eight lying on its side, to represent Wood.

Magic spells are not bestowed by supernatural powers. The only force capable of doing so is the will. Beseeching malevolent or benevolent dieties is merely a request to let yourself please yourself.

Magic spells do confer magic powers, but these powers are the result of patience, practice, and perseverance on the part of the seeker, to learn and memorize the components and materials needed, to select the symbols of greatest significance, and to assemble them for ritual performance. Obviously, consultation with other experts and a certain amount of note-taking is required until one becomes familiar with the principles of magic.

Spells work in direct proportion to the number of times they have been successful and the significance of their component symbols. The effective range of a spell is determined by the level of skill of the operator. The more experience and power one can generate and transmit, the greater the efficacy of the magic.

Most spells operate only within the sphere of influence— that is to say, inside the imaginary shell of energy that surrounds the body, like an aura, at about arm's length. Some spells require physical contact—touch—to be effective; some a personal item of the object of the spell, imprinted with its genetic code.

Duration is also affected by the ability of the spell caster. Generally speaking, a spell, once cast, lasts as long as concentration upon it is held. Likewise, the amount of time required to launch such an effect, including the preparation and arrangement of the components, is reduced with practice. Some spells work immediately, others take a little time.

Some spells don't work on some people. Strong emotions, such as anger or fear, can prevent a purely mental effort to bring about change. Love is the strongest force. A spell motivated by love cannot fail, nor can any spell overcome true love.

All spells are reversible, whether by the spell caster himself or through reflection by a stronger will.

Bear in mind that terms such as "magic spell" are only words. They are not the sinister or evil techniques so often associated with magic but merely another way of describing a perfectly natural and logical ability possessed by all human beings.

THE AURA

Just as the atmosphere of the earth is held around the planet by electromagnetic and gravitational forces, so too are the charged particles that are the products of respiration. There is an "aura" of gaseous particles around the body. This is analogous to the scent that surrounds humans and is perceptible primarily to dogs, with their more highly developed sense of smell. In some cases, a malodorous smell can even be detected by the normal human nose as well.

If all this is true, then why not an electromagnetic field as well? Certainly, the minuscule particles possess some charge, simply by being composed of atoms made of electrons, protons, and neutrons. If we accept that nerve impulses, although produced by chemical interaction, are essentially electrical in nature, then it logically follows that they, too, must produce some inductive field that extends beyond the physical nerve itself. Every other electrical current produces such a field.

Without a doubt there is an aura, and it is perceptible to some gifted or skilled people. It is alterable according to respiration and mood, as previously shown.

The purpose of the mental exercise that follows is to fill that aura with charged particles released through normal respiration but more highly charged by breathing, so that the sphere of influence (aura) becomes opaque, like a clear glass filled with smoke. The effect is to render the user "invisible" to himself, which generates the body language and mental attitude to render him or her "invisible" to others.

There is an inherent difficulty when employing this method: namely, if one cannot see one's hands or feet, there is a tendency to bump into things and knock them over. For this reason, the Ninja train in blindfold techniques; the techniques that arise spontaneously are very similar to those used by the blind. It may seem paradoxical that moving around as if you were blind would contribute to making you invisible to others, but the psychological effect of diminishing the ego to the point where you can't even see your own hand allows you to focus all of your attention on those other people and remain out of their line of sight. Also, because of this intense concentration, you (like a blind man) would logically be more likely to stumble into something and betray your presence.

THE SPELL OF INVISIBILITY

The exercise (spell) that follows confers upon the spell caster the singular ability to become invisible at will such that his presence will not be detected by normal sight or even sophisticated sensing devices. It does not affect is body mass or physical manifestation. The user still has weight and occupies space: he can still make boards creak by walking on them. Thus, there is still a need for silence.

It does overcome the problem of H. G. Wells's Invisible Man, who found that food was visible inside of his stomach until it had been digested, because, as indicated above, the body is not transparent but rather enshrouded in the mist or cloud. As it is still solid, however, it does cast a shadow and leave footprints like Wells's character.

This spell remains extant for as long as the will holds it in place. The best practice is absolute stillness, i.e., meditation. Even the breathing must be quiet to the point where it cannot be heard by the seeker. One measure of how long the Invisibility Spell will last is to count your heartbeats while holding your breath. Actually, the lungs are held empty, that is to say, no inhalation is made after the exhalation that begins this test. Most people can't hold their breath for more than thirty seconds, about forty heartbeats (at the rate of seventy-two beats per minute for men and eighty beats per minute for women, on the average). With practice, however, the time can be extended to one hundred beats. The ancient texts on Ninja medicine say that if one can hold the breath for this long, one is halfway to immortality. Bear in mind that this is not intended as a means to stay "invisible" for long periods. A few moments' application at the proper time is the key to "clouding men's minds."

Remember, however, that there is a price to be paid for every magical work. In black magic schools this is often blood, which is usually one of the ingredients necessary to complete an incantation. On the psychological level, this is an indication of the magician's desperation and his willingness to sacrifice to achieve his goal. In Ninjitsu, the price is the promise to teach these mysteries to ten others. Finding ten who are worthy and capable may take a lifetime. Therefore, do not use these devices frivolously or for too long. As Wells's protagonist in his *Invisible Man* and the antagonists in Tolkien's *Hobbit* found, absolute power does corrupt absolutely.

Place the index finger of your right hand to your lips and whisper the syllable "*shhh*" as if asking someone to be quiet. In Chinese medicine, this sound is associated with the lungs. It is said that pronouncing this syllable helps to dispel fear—and this is so.

Have you ever seen accident victims who were calmed by a comforting hand and someone whispering softly that everything was going to be all right? Human beings instinctively make this sound when cooing at or quieting a baby. Whether the child becomes programmed to the relaxation response elicited by this cue or recognizes it as the sound of respiration, a certain sign of life despite pain or discomfort, is quite irrelevant. That it calms the person is the important factor. Likewise, it has a calming effect on the speaker.

The finger-to-lips gesture is also universally recognized to mean a request for silence. Some mystery schools teach that the thumb should be used, but this places the Vertical Fist directly in front of the face, making it more of a threat than a request. This gesture can be seen over great distances and, when coupled with a stern expression and strong eye contact, can actually serve as a nonverbal reprimand quite effectively. From a psychological perspective, it turns the onlooker to whom it is directed into a coconspirator of silence—and all the more so, the longer he waits to disobey.

With the fingertip to the lips forming the Mudra of the Silent Way, inhale slowly, deeply, and silently three times. On the first exhalation, imagine three horizontal lines, one above the other. They represent Heaven, Earth, and Man, just as in the Juice of Jade Exercise. On the second exhalation, imagine only two lines remaining, and on the third, only one.

At the conclusion of the third exhalation, swallow. Touch the tip of your tongue to the roof of your mouth and mentally recite a short, calming phrase or prayer, using the Self-Hypnosis Technique to reinforce the desired result.

Phrases such as "I am now completely relaxed," or "I am at a deeper, healthier, level of consciousness," are in this way associated mentally with the ritual of the relaxation response.

Likewise, a similar phrase, such as, "I am better," or "I am returning to full waking consciousness," should be used when coming out of the trance. This helps separate the meditation experience from the stress of the day, making it a refuge and a sanctuary against the pressures of daily life. The Japanese have used it for centuries to restore balance to their lives—and so can anyone who practices it. The effects are cumulative and require diligent practice at first, but the benefits are well worth the effort.

Release the mudra and form instead the Eight Channels Mudra. This connects the channels of energy within the body. They are like the meridians of acupuncture, lymph circulation, or blood vessels—natural pathways of circulation.

This finger-knitting position, like all of those in the Kuji Kiri system, is used to connect the systems of the body in a specific arrangement so that healing or similar facets of "magic" can be performed. (For a fuller discussion, read my *Secrets of the Ninja*, Citadel Press, 1981.)

The Eight Psychic Channels run up the back, down the front of the body, around the waist, down the insides of the arms, up the backs of the arms, down the outsides of the legs, up the insides of the legs to the Tan T'ien, and up the center of the torso to solar plexus level. For this reason all schools of meditation begin with focus on the Hara, or Tan T'ien.

When you are sitting with legs crossed, the mudra to unite these channels in their most efficient arrangement is to connect the middle finger to the thumb and place the palms face up on the knees. You need not think of the circulation for it to occur, although there are texts and schools that teach the conscious direction of the Force. If you merely sit long enough, you will learn everything you need to know.

As before, the back should be straight, the shoulders square, and the eyes closed, looking easily at the tip of the nose. Inhale slowly and deeply, filling the Tan T'ien with Qi. Imagine the flame upon which you concentrated in the earlier chapter to be a small, warm, friendly fire, in the Golden Stove of the Hara, filling the body with warmth, light, and life, much as a hearth fills a home.

Let the saliva you swallowed as you counted—three, two, one—be the Juice of Jade, as it fills the cauldron and is warmed and evaporated into a steamy mist by the heat of the internal Fire. This is the mystical essence of the Cloud. Tighten the Hara and let it rise up the spine to the skull, where it condenses as golden drops of dew, the Yod symbol of the Egyptian Tarot Deck. This is the internal distillation process, exactly like the one used to distill the essence of herbs into elixirs or corn into "moonshine" liquor. These drops of dew are the refined essence of the Juice of Jade. Although they are spoken of here in allegorical symbolism, they also exist chemically and can be activated by mental imagery. They are the elixir of life.

THE MIST

Exhale slowly and without effort. Imagine a blue-white vapor or mist, which is the "steam" of the internal distillation process, being emitted with the exhalation as you whisper, "Shhh." Let it descend and cover your legs, swirling softly to form a haze or fog around your lower body, like a warming blanket. Feel the relaxation in every part of the body as it slowly envelops the physical self. It feels good to be relaxed. It feels better than before.

Repeat this procedure nine times, letting the Cloud build until you are completely engulfed and oblivious to the outside world, forming an impenetrable shield held within the sphere of influence, the aura, by force of will, like filling a glass with water.

Creating the Mist (A)

Form the Mudra of the Silent Way by placing your index finger to your lips with your little finger extended and the middle and ring fingers curled into the palm.

Creating the Mist (A)

Creating the Mist (B)

Creating the Mist (B)

Inhale and draw air into the Golden Stove. Circulate it eighty-one times using the Nine Breaths, forming the Eight Channels Mudra with both hands.

Creating the Mist (C)

Creating the Mist (D)

Creating the Mist (C)

Imagine vapor being expelled on each exhalation, descending to form a mist or fog which settles about the body, and then begins to rise and evaporate, spreading itself upon the wind. Imagine the cloud becoming more dense as it fills the "auric egg"—the electromagnetic field of the body.

Creating the Mist (D)

Imagine becoming part of the Cloud as it surrounds the body completely, obscuring the form from view. Imagine the body becoming lighter and lighter until it is carried away with the dissipating mist, so that the form vanishes completely and cannot be seen.

Imagine the Cloud itself dispersing until it, too, is lost to the sight and achieves absolute invisibility, becoming "one with the Universe," as the old ones would describe it. Time and space have no meaning. One is impervious to heat or cold, beyond the tactile level of reality, where anything is possible, a dream state.

The aborigines of Australia have a great lore regarding this dream-time that is well worth investigating. The essence, however, is to link memory with imagination. Then one can visualize, or imagine, the outcome of any scenario or the solution to any puzzle. It will be presented to him in terms and symbols completely understandable to him, some of which are archetypal and some of which are personal.

You are your own best teacher, and the only one worthy to be your master. Let no man say otherwise.

INVISIBILITY

One can move about slowly when surrounded by the mist, or Cloud, and so perform acts of the Will invisibly. In meditation, the initial stages of practice, this movement is known as the internal work, the healing and detoxifying of the body by collecting, cultivating, and circulating the Qi, or life force. In a physical sense, moving about means to "ride the wind"—that is to say, let yourself move so slowly and quietly and spontaneously in response to the actions or line of sight of others that you become "one with Nature," part of the background that is overlooked—invisible. This enables the Ninja to not be seen and not attract attention until he is ready to "step out of the mist" and suddenly appear to the enemy. Silence is the key. When you can breathe so slowly and deeply that you cannot hear yourself, then you can move slowly and quietly enough to be invisible. You will also have developed the patience needed to do so.

Slowness is of major importance. Think of how every movement inside a real cloud would disturb the gaseous mist and threaten to expose an arm or hand to view. Practice moving in water or imagine that you are doing so to elicit the necessary visual image.

Any attack you launch while invisible has a 50 percent better chance of success and does twice the damage, since the opponent is unprepared and has no chance to defend himself by rolling with the punch, making an effective block, or steeling himself against impact. Naturally, any such aggressive behavior negates the concentration required to remain "invisible," thus breaking the "spell" and making the magician "visible."

This is why invisible actions are always more subtle and employ very little force. In Tai Chi Chuan, it is said that a "force of one thousand pounds may be deflected by four ounces," and in Pa Kua Chang it is taught that to "affect the lives of men, one must be outside the circle that presses them." Both of these principles are part of Invisible Fist philosophical teaching. The greatest warrior wins without throwing a punch.

It is, of course, not necessary to move about when surrounded by the mist. It is perfectly permissible to merely sit and enjoy the sensation of relaxation and solitude. While in this state, it is possible to effect the self-healing of old wounds and injuries by merely thinking them well.

There are many schools and methods used for this practice— too many to enumerate here. Suffice it to say that if one tries this one will develop a system and a suitable set of mental techniques without need of any further instruction whatsoever. It may help, however, to consult with other wizards or healers to save time or confirm that the methods are in fact in keeping with the principles of magic, meditation, or even prayer. If they work, they are correct. It is as simple as that.

RETURN TO EARTH

Dispel the mist gradually by "blowing it away." Exhale gently, whispering the syllable, "Whoo."

This is the sound of the Earth, represented in Chinese medicine by the stomach and the spleen. It is only natural that one should use the sound symbolic of the earth to return to Earth—or to return to consciousness—if you prefer the clinical term, after this mental exercise.

As the breath and sound move away, they will carry the fog with them, and visibility will return gradually. One should not come out of the autohypnotic state suddenly. At first, it will be hard to even sit still. Then it will be difficult to imagine the Cloud at all, but with perseverance, patience, and practice, it can be done.

It might be hard to dispel the vapor, making it necessary to whisper the "who" (Hu) mantra as many times as needed to produce the fog with the "shhh" sound—perhaps nine.

After a while, the Cloud will be more easily dispelled. That is to say, in only three breaths or one, depending on the depth of concentration. These three then can be used to count up from the relaxed state, just as counting backwards, three to one, was used to induce it. Counting up to return to full wakefulness and alertness, feeling better than before, is a positive awakening ritual that brings with it the feeling of warmth and relaxation produced by the practice of invisibility.

Just visualize three horizontal lines, one above the other, the Chinese ideogram for the number three, taking them off from top to bottom as you go deeper, and replacing them from the bottom when waking up. Swallow and release the tongue from connecting the Jen Mo and To Mo channels of the body. Forgot about that mnemonic device, didn't you? That is one reason Ninjitsu is called the Silent Way, because you can't talk when your tongue is on the roof of your mouth.

Then, relax by sighing, or remain in a meditative state for some other mental exercise and later on return to full waking consciousness by counting the lines upward or just imagining the numbers as you rouse yourself.

As previously stated, some concluding phrase or benediction should be rendered to separate the solitary cultivation of energy from mundane reality. Some schools use "Om," a sixty-cycle harmonic, or its variations, like "Amen." Magicians like "So" as a conclusionary remark: "So let it be written, so let it be done..."

IN THE MIST OF BATTLE

Use your mist as part of the "power to cloud men's minds" in combat. As your attacker makes his challenge, imagine the Cloud in which you meditate building in the Hara, or lower belly. Tighten the lower belly and blow a puff of air gently at his face, just as in the Empty Hand Breath-Weapon in the first chapter. This time the Qi, in the vapor, is being projected with it, just as you would to snuff out a candle in any of the exercises given. The flame is imagined to be directly above and between his brows. This is the Third Eye technique used by hypnotists to fix the gaze of the subject. You do not have to blow hard enough to make him blink—only enough to "think" the cloud around his head, dimming and smothering the candle flame of his will.

Projecting the mist at the enemy

Projecting the Mist at the Enemy

As you exhale the puff of air at him, tighten the belly still further and open your mouth so that you can exhale from the solar plexus. Expand your chest, a subtle "puffing up" gesture, and lean forward slightly as you follow the puff with a long "Haaa," breathing the heat of the inner fire at the face of the enemy. "Show your fangs" by baring the teeth somewhat and look at him as if the human torch was setting his head on fire. This is the Fire Breathing Ninja Technique. He should feel the heat of your breath and perceive that you are about to make a kill-or-be-killed response to his challenge, which may give him pause to reconsider if it is worth it. If he breaks stance or falls back, the battle is won. If not, jump on him or vanish while he tries to decide if you are insane—or not!

INVISIBLE FISTS

Dragon Palm Fist

As we have discussed, all of the Ninja magic techniques operate on all levels simultaneously: visual, auditory, and kinesthetic. The Ninja of old often used subtle gestures to identify themselves to each other when acting under cover. One of these, which indicated that the agent was advanced to the level of skill that enabled him to perform this spell of invisibility, was the Dragon Palm Fist. In combat, this gesture may be used to intimidate the enemy on a subconscious level or warn him that he is about to be struck by one skilled in the Invisible Fist. In black magic schools this hand sign is called the Cornu, or devil's horns.

Dragon Palm Fist

It should be noted that the Dragon Palm Fist of Chinese martial arts is made by bending the middle and ring fingers into the open hand so that the index and little fingers form "dragon horns." The thumb is bent and locked to harden the fist. Strikes are made with the needle finger to the Dim Mak pressure points; by raking downward with the middle and ring fingers, which form the Dragon Claw; with the edge of the hand, as in the Swordhand Strike; with the inside edge of the palm, like a Ridgehand Strike; by hooking the thumb into the eye or mouth; or by poking both eyes with the index and little fingers.

The Dragon Palm Fist was brought to China from the Himalaya of Tibet, where it was known as the Lama Hand, the Way of the Monk. In the Black Dragon School of Ninjitsu it is Mi Chuan, the Invisible Fist, or the Hidden Hand.

Another application of this gesture is found in American Sign Language. When the back of the thumb is pressed against the heart, and the index and little fingers are extended with the middle and ring fingers folded into the palm, it forms a combination of three letters or words. *I* is formed by the little finger extended and the thumb at the heart; *you* is indicated by the index finger, which would ordinarily be pointed at the listener; and the letter *L* for *love* is made by extending the index finger with the thumb held at a right angle. It is the sign for "I love you" that is recognized worldwide. It is similar to the American Indian sign language gesture for *friend*, and to the Shaolin salute in which the Standing Palm is placed above the left, upward-turned-open palm at solar plexus level.

Standing palm   *Lama hand*

Standing Palm

The hand-to-face gesture is also a method of blocking a choke hold in Judo, and can be used psychologically in battle by placing the fist on the chin or slapping oneself with the palm. While the opponent pauses to wonder what is being evaluated or why you struck yourself, he blinks, and you are gone.

Lama Hand

The Lama Hand of Tibetan Kung Fu is the source of the lost forms of Ninjitsu and the secret teachings of the Hidden Kingdom, called Shangri-la by some, which have always been among the most esoteric. The Lama Hand is, literally, the art of overcoming any opponent, no matter how large or small, instantly, regardless of the size, age, or infirmity of the defender, with *no physical contact*. What more could one ask from a martial art?

THE MIND GATE METHOD

If Ninja are the ultimate warriors, it is because they have the knowledge and will to use the Way of the Invisible Fist.

There are many excellent fighting systems, and it is left to the individual to find for himself those techniques or styles that work best for him. To quote the late Bruce Lee, "Absorb what is useful." That does not mean that everyone will absorb the same things or that what appears to be useless may not have some redeeming virtue. Nor is it our intent to insult any other martial art by saying that one is better than another. Other seekers have other paths and there are many ways of becoming "invisible."

Hsi-Men-Jitsu, the Way of the Mind Gate, is the name given to psychology in the ancient texts and sacred scrolls of the Ninja. Unlike the Dragon Method, which is essentially kinesthetic, this system is almost entirely visual. As in the Kuji Kiri meditation practice, Qi, in the Small Heavenly Cycle, having been raised through the Nine Gates of the Heavenly Pillar (spine), is circulated in the Mysterious Chamber, the skull, and is directed with the Third Eye. Control is exerted through mental imagery. One merely thinks of what he wants the enemy to do and it is done. Whatever can be imagined can be accomplished. This is very similar to the Tantric teachings and the use of the dream state in problem-solving exercises.

Those who vanish by this method normally do so by turning the eyes upward in their sockets to look at the Third Eye between the brows. Those who have witnessed such a demonstration report that room lights begin to dim, then darkness fills the room so that only a spot of light can be seen on the forehead of the yogi. When this is gone, all is blackness: practical invisibility. As amazing as this may seem, it, like the

Dragon Method, is based on practical, physical laws and also operates on many levels. Two of these should be explained.

First, you can't hide what you can't see. While the Dragon Technique affects the eyes and surrounds the user with a mist, the Mind Gate Method functions by simply making it impossible to see. Masters of this art can place the idea of the fist into the mind of an opponent and excel at the skills of both hypnotism and illusion.

Second, on the physical level, the application of this technique can be as simple as turning out a light. The eye reacts to the change in available light by expanding or contracting the pupil. This takes a finite amount of time. For those seconds when this process is in effect, one cannot see clearly. In a desperate situation, knocking over a lamp to produce such darkness is permissible.

By the same token, a sudden flash of light makes the iris constrict, producing temporary blindness. Ordinary flashbulbs can be made to go off to make one see spots before the eyes without the need of a camera or other large apparatus. Imagine, a flashcube as a self-defense weapon! Yet, we all know how effective they are at making us blink or squint.

Those who have been "struck" by followers of the Mind Gate have said they see a flash of light so bright that it makes them recoil instinctively. Those who have experienced the Dragon Method can actually feel its impact. *Haraki* victims speak of pressure in the ears or a sound so high-pitched as to cause pain.

SUMMONING DEMONS FROM WITHIN

The Demon Mask School of Ninjitsu holds that to present a terrifying image to the enemy is often a useful psychological ploy that may even dissuade him from further aggression— much like the stern look of a parent when hushing a child or the contorted scream of a martial artist as he hurls himself into battle. To this end, they devised elaborate costumes and masks made of bone or used bright red colors or fangs to frighten their enemies. Many of these were patterned after the symbolic costumes of the Japanese Noh Plays, which are specifically designed to elicit an emotional response from the audience. This practice is analogous to the use of skulls and other alchemical symbols by some mystery schools to discourage interest in their techniques.

Demon mask with spirit shout

Demon Mask With Spirit Shout

Kata Dan'te, as taught in the Black Dragon Fighting Society, is similar in concept and application. It combines the spirit shout, also known as the Exhaling Breath of *Kiai*, to tighten the body against injury and launch an attack of total commitment at the enemy, who is paralyzed by the ferocity and the sudden shout, enabling the Ninja to prevail. Part of this training is to release all bottled-up fear and anger produced by daily stress into the shout. Imagine it as a ball of fire being blasted from your belly, engulfing and destroying the object of your hatred or fear. That is the Fire-Breathing Dragon! It is also the primal scream, a purging of negative thoughts and emotions, and it generates the courage to stand up for yourself. If you "see" it, so will your opponent. He will feel the heat of your anger and fear your wrath, and you will prevail.

DISTRACTION

All of these things are what a magician would call distractions, or misdirection. A boxer would think of them as fakes or feints, used to create an opening in an opponent's defenses. If this can be done by breaking the concentration of the opponent, the Ninja can launch his attack, or flee invisibly. Simple tricks like tossing a coin behind a sentry will often make him turn to investigate the odd noise. Looking over the shoulder of an opponent gives him the impression that there is someone behind him.

In Kung Fu, many styles teach how to simultaneously attack two targets, gambling that one will succeed if the other fails, making it all the more difficult for the opponent to read the incoming attack and mount an adequate defense. In Ninjitsu, the technique of attacking a heavily defended passageway to draw enemy troops away from the surreptitious entry of a single agent or team at some more remote site has long been a stratagem of battle, just as has been the trick of throwing crude gunpowder into a campfire to make a blinding flash of smoke and light.

Anything which can be used to make an enemy blink can and probably has been employed at one time or another. It only takes a second to duck out of sight.

PATIENCE, SILENCE

We have no fear that these techniques will be misused or perverted, since those who would do such things do not have the patience or perseverance to learn them. You can know the secret of the Fire-Breathing Dragon and still not be able to perform it due to lack of confidence resulting from inadequate preparation. You can learn the secret mudra that confers the power of Invisibility, but unless you have done all that is explained herein, slowly, step-by-step, there is no way the technique will ever work for you.

There are things that can only be learned by doing them, and lessons will be learned along the way. No one can tell you all of these things. They must be found out for oneself. Thus, they are presented in the manner of self-instruction.

We want or need no followers, no devotees, no ardent admirers. We want each person to be the best he or she can possibly be. There are no masters in the ranks of the Ninja. We believe that one should have many teachers and try many styles, the better to find the truth for oneself and to train oneself to be one's own master. Part of that is developing the self-confidence of knowing you can defend yourself—by becoming invisible if need be.

We are not a club, team, or army. We are a fraternity of like-minded individuals—friends who help each other and set a good example for others.

Now that you have learned the secret teaching—the Yin, or dark side, of the Silent Way—do you understand why it is called that? Because the entire system is based on the physio-psychological response elicited by placing the fingertip to the lips and saying, "Shhh..."

The secret of staying invisible is Silence.

Now do you understand why it was kept secret? Because it is so easy! There are no gymnastics, no tumbling, no death blows or gore. No years of brutal training under stern Sensei or paying for lessons.

Anyone having read this book can defend himself or herself with a handful of sand. These are methods even the most extreme pacifist could endorse. They are as nonviolent as the fighting arts are savage and terrifying. Yet each has its place and applications.

Even for the Invisible Tribe, as the wheel of life continues to revolve, one will be faced with problems, obstacles, or confrontations with those who believe that violence is the answer to everything, and for them it is.

"Do unto others as you would have them do unto you" is more than a maxim. It is also an explanation of human psychology. If a man comes to you and wants to beat you up, this means that *he*, for some reason, wishes to be beaten. There are many motivations for this behavior, but they are of little consequence. If he wants a whipping, the Ninja is usually capable of providing it, but since the Ninja reveres all life, he will go to almost any lengths to avoid having to fight. In attempting to live as a superior man, the goal of the *I Ching*, the Book of Changes, and set a good example for all, he will run, hide, and accept verbal abuse and slander without striking back. Only when there is no escape, when trapped, when the stakes are life-and-death does he permit himself to use the savage and terrifying fighting arts of which he is capable.

Some schools of invisibility teach that one must become nondescript, anonymous, lost in the crowd. It is essentially the principle of attracting no interest. They instruct that one should practice by staring into a mirror until a field of shimmering energy manifests itself between the observer and the observed. This curtain of noninterest is faint and indescribable, except to say it appears, as do the distortions produced by heat rising from a road to create a mirage in the desert—a bending of light rays by an area of heated air, which acts as a natural lens. Not as fantastic as it sounded earlier, is it?

The Koga Hai Lung Ryu (Black Dragon School) of Ninjitsu performs this feat by filling the "sphere of influence," the aura, with a fog or mist—a vapor that conceals the Ninja from view, as explained. What is seen within the Cloud, in the mind, is not seen clearly at first. The Ninja must remain in the quiet places that attract no interest, lest his presence be felt or otherwise sensed. This is called *kobudera*, "the masking of real intent."

Some say the substance from which the Cloud is formed is called *akasa* and collects in the corners with the dust that is harvested to fill the *hai lan*, or black eggs, used to vanish as described in "The Book of Earth." This magical dust is analogous to the pixie dust magicians claim is found in the linty corners of almost any pocket and can be sprinkled on objects to make them do extraordinary things. The real trick is that when he dips into his pocket for the pixie dust he is also dropping off the object in question.

Like the dust-harvesting process itself, the psychological effect is that of mentally gathering the Qi to fill the aura, making it opaque, as opposed to transparent. Then there are those who believe that the "power to cloud men's minds" can be wholly generated from within. These are the followers of the Fire Breathing Dragon School.

The first step, Kindling the Fire in the Belly, is the first exercise in the development of this power. Collecting the Qi in the Center, refining it with the imaginary heat of the Golden Stove (cultivation), and letting the "steam" produced by the boiling Juice of Jade rise to the brain is always the initial stage. How else could one hope to breathe fire on an opponent and defeat him with the same energy that enables Hindu yogis to walk on burning coals or fast for weeks at a time?

This practice confers control of the "reptile" brain, the brain stem in every human being concerned with survival and response to environmental stimuli. To the yogis it is *kundalini*, the "serpent-power" that represents sexual energy. To the Ninja, it is Hou Lung Qi, the Way of the Fire Breathing Dragon.

THE SWORD THAT DOES NOT KILL

The quest for invisibility is only one road that leads to the top of the mountain of knowledge and understanding offered by many others. The same chants, guidelines, and symbols serve as signposts and mile markers along the gradual learning process of perfecting the Self.

Those who seek out this knowledge do so because they think attaining it is impossible, and, if they could do something impossible, it would provide some clue to understanding all the other things that elude them—that are "invisible"—without adequate explanation. When they find out how something is done, they either don't have the patience to do it properly or are disappointed because it is so simple it is hard to believe it would fool anyone, especially them—but it can, and does.

As promised, even the most meek and mild among you, even the most passive and nonviolent, can find a way to defend yourself and have self-esteem—if not with these exact techniques, then by adapting these principles to your own needs.

It was said that Miyamoto Musashi, the most famous swordsman of feudal Japan, had engraved on one side of the hand guard of his sword "The Sword That Kills" and on the other side "The Sword That Spares Life." It would be interesting to know which face was presented to the enemy and which to himself.

For the Hai Lung Ryu, it is the Invisible Fist that does not kill.